WORDS *and* MUSIC

WORDS *and* MUSIC

Confessions of an Optimist

STEPHEN RUBIN

APPLAUSE
THEATRE & CINEMA BOOKS
Essex, Connecticut

APPLAUSE
THEATRE & CINEMA BOOKS

An imprint of Globe Pequot, the trade division of
The Rowman & Littlefield Publishing Group, Inc.
4501 Forbes Blvd., Ste. 200
Lanham, MD 20706
www.rowman.com

Distributed by NATIONAL BOOK NETWORK

British Library Cataloguing in Publication Information available

Library of Congress Cataloging-in-Publication Data

Names: Rubin, Stephen E., author.
Title: Words and music : confessions of an optimist / Stephen Rubin.
Description: Essex, Connecticut : Applause Press, [2022]
Identifiers: LCCN 2022012415 (print) | LCCN 2022012416 (ebook) | ISBN
    9781493065103 (cloth) | ISBN 9781493065110 (epub)
Subjects: LCSH: Rubin, Stephen E. | Publishers and publishing—Biography. |
    Journalists—Biography. | Music critics—Biography. | LCGFT:
    Autobiographies.
Classification: LCC Z473.R795 A3 2022 (print) | LCC Z473.R795 (ebook) |
    DDC 070.5092 [B]—dc23/eng/20220713
LC record available at https://lccn.loc.gov/2022012415
LC ebook record available at https://lccn.loc.gov/2022012416

♾™ The paper used in this publication meets the minimum requirements of American National Standard for Information Sciences—Permanence of Paper for Printed Library Materials, ANSI/NISO Z39.48-1992

For Karen,
I miss you every day.

CONTENTS

FOREWORD

For years friends and colleagues have been urging me to write my autobiography. My response to them has always been that, as a publisher, I know how poorly such a book would sell and my ego could not tolerate it.

This has been something of a ruse. I realize that I have had a compelling career populated with colorful, prominent personalities. And I know how to tell a good yarn.

What actually stopped me from proceeding was the reason I often find autobiographies such a slog. Too many details about uninteresting things, childhood, adolescence, and so forth. Finally, I woke up to the obvious fact that I could write a memoir and include whatever I pleased. Then I refined it further: I would write a "professional" memoir and dispense entirely with personal stuff, which is nobody's business anyway. I pretty much stuck to this disposition and broke it only when necessary, as when my wife Cynthia's career and mine intermingled, or when I had a momentous professional opportunity, like relocating to London, which I never would have accepted without her support. I also have to acknowledge that Cynthia and I had a shared passion for words and music that to a certain degree fueled and perhaps even defined our wonderfully sunny 45-year relationship.

Very secretly I began to write. I hired a research assistant, and he was able to find all the myriad articles I had written when I was a journalist, and then printed reams of clips from the start of my publishing career through the publication of *The Da Vinci Code*. Most important, he supplied a list of the books Doubleday had published during my years there, until I decamped for

London. All of this research was invaluable, particularly in igniting a foggy memory.

When I had what I thought was a representative number of pages, I asked the formidable UK agent Clare Alexander and the distinguished publisher Jonathan Galassi to read them. Was I in for a surprise. Both essentially said the same thing: while they found the pages entertaining, it was much too journalistic and needed to be opened up to feel more like a book rather than an article. I understood exactly what they meant but had very little confidence that I could deliver what they were asking for, and it stopped me cold.

More than a decade later, I returned to the pages and began what turned out to be a joyful experience of rewriting the entire damn thing. I finally understood why so many splendid writers whom I have published say that rewriting is the part of the writing they enjoy the most.

I should also say that I tried very hard not to be the hero of every story, to vividly recollect some of my most notorious, appalling blunders, either with acquisitions or personnel. I have spared no one, including myself. There is definitely news in these pages and also plenty of gossip. I just wonder if anybody cares after so many years. We shall see.

1
KID STUFF

Even as a lad, I was headstrong. During my preteen years my mother suggested that I embark upon the noble endeavor of all middle-class Jewish kids: piano lessons. I instantly rejected the notion. Piano lessons are what all the kids do, I whined. I wanted to do something different, something special, like art lessons. I wanted to learn how to draw.

The irony of this obstinate, youthful blunder is that I had zero talent for drawing but had an innate and invincible feeling and passion for music. Still, I am convinced that had I taken piano lessons as a kid, my approach to music as an adult would have been hamstrung by the rigid observance of the rules, as opposed to the freewheeling, openhearted manner in which I responded to music as a child.

Such was my enthusiasm for music, my mother took a deep bow and told anyone who would listen that my dedication to things musical was all because she had WQXR, New York's prime classical radio station, on full blast when I was a toddler in my high chair.

Maybe she was right. I remember receiving cash as a bar mitzvah present and going straight to the Sam Goody record store to buy Andre Kostelanetz's orchestral synthesis of Bizet's *Carmen*. Happily, my musical sophistication has vastly improved since then.

I remember my first opera vividly: *The Tales of Hoffmann*, at the Metropolitan, when I was 12. Not only was I enchanted by Offenbach's fanciful and easily accessible score and the dramatic goings-on onstage, but the night I attended was a benefit for the United Jewish Appeal, and a good number of the audience members were fartootsed to the nth. The ladies wore expensive, gaudy ensembles, probably from Bergdorf Goodman, the flashier the better. Their mostly overweight husbands stuck to suits and ties, the latter no doubt from swanky Sulka. To be perfectly frank, I cannot tell you what impressed me more, the gussied-up Jews or the phantasmagorical developments on the giant Met stage.

As for those art lessons, in two years of weekly lessons with a fetching instructor, the most I accomplished was a life-size rendering of a piggy bank. I rest my case.

It wasn't until I was an undergraduate that I evinced an interest in the written word by joining the *Square Journal,* New York University's college newspaper, as a reviewer of live and recorded classical music performances. I had no more right judging these endeavors than flying to the moon, but you would never know it from the know-it-all manner of my opinionated articles.

It embarrasses me to recount this, but in a review I wrote of a performance of *Tosca* at the Met, I had no idea that the choral section that closes the first act is a Te Deum. Blessedly, I cannot recall how I covered up this appalling ignorance. Maybe even worse, I reviewed my very first encounter with Strauss's *Elektra* at the Met. At least I had the good taste to recognize that in Inge Borkh's interpretation of the title role, I was witnessing a searing and exhausting memorable performance. To this day, Borkh is one of my favorite singers.

Nonetheless, I used my platform at the *Square Journal* to foolishly trot out all sorts of uninformed opinions, like my irrational dislike of Debussy, which continues to this day, and to generally display my youthful arrogance. Sibelius? Not for this fellow. Britten? Only in very small doses. Bartók? Spare me, please. Of course, except in the case of Debussy, I have come to my senses about all these remarkable composers.

God knows why, but within two years I became the editor in chief of the *Square Journal*. I must have talked a very good game. But to give credit where it is due, I surely had no compunction for taking charge, making decisions, and shooting my mouth off. This was the first hint of what was to come. I seemed to have had a natural inclination for leadership, or at least a very sure sense of myself.

If my passions were divided between words and music, with music always winning pride of place, my professional leanings evolved into a dichotomous mess. What was I? Laborer or manager? Writer or editor? Worker bee or boss man?

Once I got my bearings in publishing by the mid-1980s, there were definitely no issues about who I am: boss.

I never had a strategic plan for my advancement. A lot of my success involved luck, being in the right place at the right time, and surely undaunted chutzpah.

I was a lazy student in high school, paying far more attention to reading voguish fiction than to books of substance, and I surely had no qualifications for reviewing those concerts and recordings other than a fiercely opinionated nature. But honestly, I think I viewed these freshman critical exercises as much as a means of grubbing freebies as a way of expressing myself.

I soon added books to my beat and quickly smoked out how easy it was to get them gratis. And then I made a mind-blowing discovery: The Strand, the fabled downtown Manhattan bookstore, a stone's throw from NYU's Greenwich Village campus, bought reviewer's copies of books.

Now not only did I have an endless supply of free books, but I also sorted out where I could sell them.

After two years, when I ascended to the post of editor in chief, I was also experiencing a volatile emotional tumult, reflected perfectly in my seesawing grades, vacillating between As and Ds. It was clear that I needed help.

I had been through a previous encounter with analysis when I was a very nervous preteen kid and was shipped off to a child psychiatrist. I disliked her intensely and this attitude surely didn't help our weekly sessions. One of the reasons for my displeasure with her was that she always took my side against my parents. I just felt she was unfair. For instance, my father complained that I spent too much money on ties, and was he right, but she responded that her husband spent considerably more on cravats. Huh? She was a disaster.

But this time I was older and realized that despite my success at the *Square Journal*, something was seriously amiss. Call it nonspecific anxiety. With the blessings of my incredibly supportive and generous parents, I auditioned a number of shrinks and finally embarked on Freudian analysis, three times a week, at 25 bucks a shot. The doctor's gloomy office was at 86th Street and Park Avenue, requiring me to travel uptown by subway and causing my staff to become very suspicious. "Where do you disappear to in the afternoons?" I was regularly asked. It was definitely not fashionable in the sixties, even in swinging Greenwich Village, to announce that you were seeing a headshrinker.

I stuck with this strict Freudian for almost two years. I cannot imagine how I got through it. He was humorless; his specialty was suicide in Scandinavia. An uncompromising disciple of the Viennese master, he allowed for zero give-and-take. If I asked a question, like "Why am I on the couch instead of the chair?" he would respond with another question. "Why do you think you are?" Four sessions later I had no answer.

The dour fellow asked me to keep a pad by my bed so I could write down my dreams. Dreams were my savior: something to talk about. The only time he ever behaved like a normal conversationalist was when I blurted out, "I think I am cracking up. I listen to *Cavalleria Rusticana* a couple of times a day." "Wait until you discover *Così Fan Tutte*," the taciturn shrink announced from behind left field.

When I finally told him it was time for us to stop my analysis, he asked why.

I shook his hand and thanked him for making me a reasonably sane person. His response floored me: "Maybe you just grew up!"

Under my tutelage the *Square Journal* became a laughingstock of the college newspaper world. We were roundly dissed as "the *Herald Tribune* wannabes." This was completely justified—I had a giant crush on Clay Felker's fabulous *Trib* and insisted that we look not like some crappy collegian rag, but like a tony, outright rip-off of the daily *Trib*. The *Tribune* looked gorgeous, never to be confused with the gray *New York Times*, and had a mouthwatering array of exceptional writers, like Tom Wolfe, Gloria Steinem, and Jimmy Breslin. I honestly believe that I was far more interested in our appearance and how we were perceived than in how we covered the news. Maybe that says something about me, which is reflected to a much lesser degree in who I am today.

I will never forget the first-time thrill of having to rip up the front page when John Kennedy was assassinated. Our headline read "The First Citizen of the World Is Dead"—pretty heady stuff for a bunch of teenagers.

Such was my undying commitment to the *Square Journal* that I registered only for courses that wouldn't conflict with my responsibilities at the paper. This worked to my advantage at least one semester when, between noon and 1:30, I attended a course on Jane Austen and Anthony Trollope that changed my life, at least in terms of my literary taste.

I was entirely beguiled by Trollope. *The Way We Live Now* used to be my all-time favorite novel—until I reread it about a decade ago and it broke my heart to realize it wasn't nearly as fabulous as I thought upon first blush. It just didn't feel as exciting or credible the second time around.

Of course I adored then and still do today *The Chronicles of Barsetshire*. But I gobbled up even the lesser works—*The Eustace Diamonds*—by this amazing, tireless, prolific writer. To my mind, Trollope was like Stephen King is today, a true chronicler, giving the reader a realistic snapshot of what life was like when they wrote.

As for Austen, I loved them all and remember thinking that *Sense and Sensibility* was like Haydn, and *Pride and Prejudice* was definitely Mozartean. I'll stick with that characterization.

My salad days at the university newspaper set the tone for my future career perfectly. While I enjoyed writing, particularly opinionated editorials—for instance a vehement and controversial rant about the profusion of pigeons shitting all over Washington Square Park, which offended readers, one of whom suggested I had just spit into the face of a statue of St. Francis of Assisi, who was associated with the patronage of animals—I was considerably more sanguine running the show.

Did I realize that then? Highly doubtful. I had a ball running the show at my college newspaper. I learned a lot about reporting, management, and leadership. But I am convinced all of this invaluable experience entered my mind subconsciously.

What I did know was that my active and productive time at the *Square Journal* persuaded me that journalism was the occupation I wanted to pursue. After NYU I went to Boston University on a partial scholarship, where I broke a school record and earned a master's degree in 11 months. I did this by refusing to take Basic Journalistic Writing, citing the fact that I was, after all, the editor in chief of my undergraduate newspaper.

What a waste of time and money and a lot of hooey. Nobody needs a master's in journalism. But what a great year it was, living in a five-flight walkup apartment on Beacon Street in lovely Back Bay, where there was nothing but a plethora of fellow collegians.

I spent the summer locked up in my shabby, two-room digs writing my thesis. BU gave its students the option of choosing a traditional or reportorial thesis. I opted for the latter and did a rigorous analysis of *Time* magazine. I wore out a thesaurus aping the alliterative *Time* style in writing a cover story on Erich Leinsdorf, then music director of the Boston Symphony Orchestra, who graciously gave me almost unlimited access to himself and the august institution.

Leinsdorf was extremely bright, opinionated, and chatty and loved to hear himself talk. He was incredibly astute about music and conducting. Better yet, he was waspish and indiscreet about the competition.

Given my many, lively sessions with the imprudent maestro, I discovered that I could be a keen, probing listener, surely a portent of things to come. Leinsdorf and I would have many dealings of a personal and professional nature in years to come. He was a nasty piece of work but hugely diverting.

Such was my frenzied focus on getting the thesis finished to be able to graduate in August, I became paranoid about a stalker coming in the window through the roof and refused to open the damn things. I was, sadly, dead serious. I had no air-conditioning and it was blistering. Finally, a pre-med student friend of mine came to visit and gave me the only tranquilizer I have ever taken, and, like magic, I opened the windows. And I finished the thesis, an early example of my tight-assed compunction to consummate whatever it is I am working on.

2
JOURNALISTIC ADOLESCENCE

Back in the Big Apple. I cannot remember how I won an internship to the *World Journal Tribune*, a shlocky amalgam of the *New York World*, the *Journal American*, and the *Herald Tribune*. The former rags were pioneers of yellow journalism, parented by Joseph Pulitzer and William Randolph Hearst. Of course the *Trib* was my beloved daily, although there was barely a hint left of its singular glory, especially in the company of these two tacky mastodons.

My first day of work, February 7, 1964, I walked into the newsroom and all the old Irish guys looked at me as if I were an interplanetary visitor. What a dreary place it was, a bargain-basement version of the *Front Page*. There was zero romance in this city room. Finally, old man Kilgallen, dad to the poisonous right-wing popular columnist Dorothy Kilgallen, said, "Okay kid, here's your first assignment. Go to the airport and cover the arrival of some British rock band who are appearing on Ed Sullivan's show on Sunday."

Talk about being set up for failure. They gave me no press credentials, no fatherly counsel, nada. Not even cab fare. But I took off for JFK anyway and immediately got a sense of the tumult at the International Arrivals Building. I looked around and didn't have a clue what to do. I was about to call it a day when I saw a friend from the film company United Artists, who, when told of my predicament, said, "Follow me."

Into the belly of the beast we went, and I will never forget what happened when the Beatles finally showed their adorable faces. The entire building shook, such was the hormonal power of the frenzied 4,000 teenage girls when they saw their heartthrobs. I have never heard a sound as deafening as the vigorous screams of those pent-up young women. The Beatles looked both delighted and baffled and maybe even frightened. Luckily, the quartet was held at bay from the minions by very strong plate glass.

When I returned to the newsroom, as a wildly energized intern, the tough old birds were shocked that I actually produced a piece, now lost of course, that had genuine reportage and plenty of local color. Boy, was I lucky! Tom Wolfe was also there, reporting for *Rolling Stone*, and wrote that such was the pandemonium, "some of the girls tried to throw themselves over a retaining wall."

My brief and not particularly revelatory introduction to the real world of newspapering was most dispiriting. The *World Journal Tribune* was about to be shut down, and it felt like those old geezers didn't give a damn about their young intern, who would be witness to their demise.

But soon I got a real job at a real, functional organization. I became a caption writer for United Press International, a great place to learn the business, as long as one didn't stay there too long. Don't think caption writing is easy: try not to misspell Carl Yastrzemski. After a year, I was promoted to head the newly established Roto Service, a small division of two charged with producing five features a week, text plus accompanying photos, designed to service the individually edited Sunday roto magazines or newspapers across the land.

It was terrifying. We were in the midst of the Vietnam War, and I would receive weekly rolls of raw film from our staff photographers on the battlefield. I frankly did not know what to do with this mass of film, and was convinced that I would reject the very photo that could win a Pulitzer Prize.

Even though I eventually became pretty adept at using an "eyeball" to look at contact sheets, I never had the confidence I needed to choose properly. After all, what the hell did I know about war coverage?

The famous AP photo of a naked young girl running screaming through the streets during the Vietnam War that won a Pulitzer was one I definitely would have passed by. In fact, I am convinced that there are numerous potential prizewinners in the long-forgotten cache of film I rejected.

I had much more confidence in establishing a feature called "Great Performers of Our Time," which thanks to the clout of UPI, gave me access to an alluring amalgam of Hollywood, Broadway, pop, and classical luminaries. I mean serious, household names like Judy Garland, Marlene Dietrich, Julie Andrews, Mary Martin, Gingers Rogers, Angela Lansbury, Robert Preston, Cesare Siepi, Renata Tebaldi, Woody Allen, Joanne Woodward, John Schlesinger, and Ethel Merman.

I may have been way over my head, not in how to deal with these superstars, which I somehow managed to handle with ease and maybe even finesse, but in how to write the interviews. Backstage at the Palace, where I was chatting to Garland, I must have inadvertently been staring at the drink in her hand when she taunted me with, "Hey kid, it's water!" I turned scarlet. Did I use the exchange in the piece? Of course not.

One day Marlene Dietrich and I were tucked into a corner banquette at a swanky midtown French restaurant. She looked sensational, and the only thing that betrayed her age were the liver spots on her hands. Very early in the interview, she leaned over, put one of those paws on top of mine, and cooed seductively, "*Vy* don't you turn off *ze* tape recorder." Off it went, and we had a fine time. Did I take notes? Of course not.

One of the many perks I had at UPI, beyond getting bottles of Chivas Regal in brown paper bags (journalistic payola), was getting an excellent pair of second-night seats to every show that opened on Broadway. This may seem very glamorous, but after a while the novelty wears off. And not only did I dread attending a show that had gotten terrible reviews, I had trouble finding someone to go with me. Often I just returned the tickets.

Because UPI did so many theater-oriented features, I also had backstage access to almost anyone I wanted, and embarrassingly enough, became something of a stage-door johnny, especially with Jill Haworth, who played Sally Bowles in the big hit *Cabaret*. Jill received rotten reviews, but to my schoolboy-crush eyes, she was excruciatingly lovely.

Jill is a Brit and, much like Sally Bowles, called everybody "dahling." She put up with my lapdog fawning attention, and we actually had lots of innocent fun.

One night before a performance, I arrived in Jill's dressing room, which was the only one on stage level. As dictated by her contract, she claimed it. Unfortunately, her costar Lotte Lenya had the same provision in her contract. The dueling divas decided to split the space and hung a schmatta in the middle to define the boundaries.

"How was your weekend, *dahling*," Jill asked as I arrived one evening. I saw the most ghastly movie, I told her, *Hurry Sundown*, in which Jane Fonda has a scene where she literally goes down on a saxophone.

"Biggest cocksucker in Hollywood," a disembodied voice from the bowels of the room croaked. It was the unmistakable baritonal Lotte Lenya.

I turned scarlet. Jill screeched with laughter.

3
CELEBRITY INTRUSIONS

It wasn't only at UPI that I had access to these brand-name celebrities. I was then living with a high-powered manager/publicist, whom I later married, and her clients very often intruded into our lives.

Cynthia and I met in 1966 when I interviewed the great Italian heartthrob basso Cesare Siepi. "Are you always this late for interviews," Cynthia blurted out as I walked in the door 15 minutes behind schedule. I immediately fell for her outspokenness and was hugely attracted to her take-no-prisoners attitude toward the entire interview process. She was clearly a singular character, and I liked her immediately for her moxie. The fact that she was many years older than me didn't for a minute dampen my enthusiasm.

Within a couple of months after the Siepi interview was published, I moved into her huge, rent-controlled studio apartment on lower Lexington Avenue (as opposed to my much smaller one-bedroom, rent-controlled flat on ugly West 14th Street).

One of the very few conflicts the new lovebirds had to confront were the needy demands of her closest client, the soprano Anna Moffo.

Anna was a homegrown superstar who hailed from Wayne, Pennsylvania. Although she was very glamorous in her Valentino couture clothes and refashioned face, and she had posh homes in New York and Italy and generally led what was then called a jet-set lifestyle, she was not Eurotrash at all. She was a genuinely good-hearted, sweet, small-town girl who took her career very seriously. Unfortunately, she was also incredibly naïve and listened to the self-destructive counsel of her husband, Mario Lanfranchi, an Italian film and theater director, who saw a meal ticket in his very beautiful, very rich wife. On the plus side, he filmed her performances, which gave her international visibility. Very much on the downside, he had her star in a soft-core porn film, which was more embarrassing than alluring. He also gave her misguided advice on what to sing. They were married for 15 years, and he was cruel and distant with her. She would often complain that he went out in the evenings to buy newspapers and didn't return for three hours. He was an odious man.

In all the years I knew Anna, I never heard her utter an unkind word about her colleagues, including the direct competition. She was a total pro, a fabulous cook, a darling gal, and, thanks to her inattentive husband, almost pathologically needy.

She and Cynthia were soul mates and sisters. My intrusion into this tight-knit circle created immediate tension because Anna called Cynthia every morning at 8 a.m. when she was in the States. "It's the 8 a.m. express," I would say as we battled for the phone. If I won, Anna was told we were at breakfast; if Cynthia got there first, I would lose her for never less than half an hour.

Because of her unusual fidelity, Cynthia and I would attend a ridiculous number of Anna's performances, particularly at the Met. I must have seen in excess of twenty performances of Anna's signature role, Violetta in *La Traviata*. One evening we ran into Fabrizio Melano, who was directing the revival of *Traviata*, and he invited us into the director's box, which is a tomb-like den at the back of the orchestra level. We could revel in Fabrizio's distress over the antics of Robert Merrill, the robust-voiced, pea-brained baritone, singing the elder Germont and constantly straying from Fabrizio's blocking, even though he had probably sung in this Cecil Beaton production more than fifty times.

I will never forget the notorious matinee performance of *Lucia di Lammermoor* broadcast nationally on the radio by the Met. Poor Anna simply could not "find" her voice; she was singing so badly, listeners were calling into the Met switchboard to complain. We were in the house, and it was painful to watch and hear Anna make a spectacle of herself desperately trying to get her act together.

At intermission Cynthia went backstage. I couldn't face her. She reported that Anna was resolute in continuing. "I will give them a mad scene they will never forget," she said. She was right for all the wrong reasons. Her mad scene was lamentable.

This was just the beginning. Anna's vocal problems continued to worsen, despite her working with many vocal coaches, including the great soprano Zinka Milanov, who grandly pronounced, "Darling, either you are gorgeous or an artist. I should know."

It was all for naught, and Anna was forced to retire from the stage. It was very sad to witness this vibrant, beautiful woman in decline. Toward the end of her last years, Anna's fantasy life flourished, but she was still the dear woman we cherished. Years after she stopped performing in public, Anna would hire a recording studio, an orchestra, and conductor, and record repertory she could never sing, like *Norma*.

Her countless recordings form an uneven legacy. But the good ones, the early recitals—a Villa-Lobos program conducted by Leopold Stokowski, a *Verdi* recital, the complete operas *Luisa Miller*, *La Rondine*, *Falstaff*, and *La Traviata*—divulge an idiomatic singer with a beautiful lyric soprano and a singular, velvety bottom register, but there will always be controversy over her attempts to scale the upper reaches of the coloratura repertory.

Another even more famous soprano who was very much in our lives was America's sweetheart Beverly Sills, who wasn't a client of Cynthia's but a close friend. In many ways, this relationship proved much more daunting. Even though Beverly was represented by Cynthia's firm, their affiliation was solely as cronies: two larger-than-life, outspoken, sassy, and smart self-made Jewish girls.

Of course, this friendship created a built-in conflict of interest for me as a journalist. I had this issue with all of Cynthia's clients, many of whom I profiled without any fallout. Everyone knew Cynthia and I were an item, but in this case, Beverly was not a personal client but a friend of whom Cynthia was inordinately fond, and as much as she was capable, Beverly returned the sentiment.

I first met Beverly in Boston, where she was singing Norina in Sarah Caldwell's Opera Company of Boston's very funny production of *Don Pasquale*. Cynthia was there in support of Caldwell and bass baritone Donald Gramm, who was singing the title role. I was there in support of my significant other.

On an evening between performances, we were summoned to a group dinner by Beverly's super WASP, Boston Brahmin husband, Peter Greenough, at a popular Cambridge restaurant, Joyce Chen's. The evening proved to be a hoot. Chen insinuated herself into our group, grabbing the diva's total attention. This wasn't only rude, but it put Beverly into an impossible situation. Chen's English was rudimentary and Beverly had to pretend that she understood her, a phony smile plastered on her face. None of us could look in their direction for fear of bursting into laughter.

Peter put an end to the proceedings when he announced what each couple's share of the hefty bill was. This caused bemused consternation since we all assumed we were guests, but we ponied up the bucks and were liberated.

Beverly and Peter were an unlikely duo, but I think they genuinely loved each other, even though she could never get over the fact that he was a loaded goy. He, on the other hand, couldn't believe that the Super WASP Stage Door Johnny had landed a seriously famous superstar, who happened to be seriously Jewish.

The story of their oddball marriage and their two disabled children, Muffy, who was born deaf, and Bucky, who had to be institutionalized, is well chronicled. Of course, one cannot say too many times what a terrible strike of fate it was that the diva had a daughter who could never hear her mother sing, even though she attended many of her performances.

When I knew Muffy, she was a lovely young woman (she died in 2016) who read lips proficiently, unless one had a beard, but who was still difficult to relate to because it was hard to understand her. I suppose to her credit, Beverly included Muffy in many social occasions, and I sat next to her at innumerable dinners. We both tried because we liked each other, but it was tough.

It was my mentioning her children in an article that caused Beverly and Peter to go ballistic. In the piece I wrote that there were those people who accused Beverly of using the tragedy of her kids to garner publicity.

I was summoned to their rambling Central Park West apartment, where Peter scolded me mercilessly: if I ever again dared to intrude upon them in such a hurtful manner, there would be no more dinners and no more bridge games. It was surreal, because first, the dinners were generally dismal affairs, and Cynthia and I were definitely on the B list. Occasionally we would get Carol Burnett or some other celebrity, but most of the time it was fellow B listers. The food was terrible, even worse when the diva herself whipped it up.

Bridge was a bit more fun because they had two tables, but no self-respecting participant would have found the level of play anything but laughable. What was preposterous was that Peter blithely thought I would be severely punished without access to these sorry occasions. We kissed and made up. Nothing changed, not the crappy food, rotten bridge, nor Peter's sanctimonious attitude.

As an artist, Beverly definitely sang and acted better than she played bridge. She was a theater animal through and through, and I think she will be remembered for her live performances more than for her recordings. I first saw her when I was a kid in high school singing in *La Traviata*, and I was immediately smitten. She radiated charisma and her light lyric voice was ideal for Violetta.

Then she was just a hardworking member of the New York City Opera, but after her triumph as Cleopatra in *Julius Caesar* in 1966, her formidable PR man Edgar Vincent, who was Cynthia's partner, masterminded her career to gigantic proportions: she was on the cover of *Newsweek*, she jousted with Johnny Carson on the *Tonight Show*, she was peripatetic.

Soon she made her *La Scala* debut, and that might have coaxed the Met, which had essentially ignored her, to dangle *The Siege of Corinth*, a rarely produced opera by Rossini, which was the vehicle of her *Scala* debut, and Beverly accepted.

Unfortunately, a lot of these momentous occasions came late in her career, after she had abused her voice by singing roles way too strenuous for her slight soprano, like *Norma* and the three queens in Donizetti's Tudor trilogy.

Cynthia and I were guests of Peter and Beverly for her Met debut. The occasion was very moving, but her singing was proof positive that she had mistreated her voice cruelly. This despite an 18-minute ovation.

Her Manon and Elizabeth in *Roberto Devereux* were indelible portrayals. She had a total identification with both characters and she imbued them with flamboyant, varied touches. Manon fit her like a glove; her transformation from country girl to glamorous courtesan was breathtaking. Queen Elizabeth was a real stretch vocally, but she was so mesmerizing onstage it didn't matter. Another triumph for her was the title character in Douglas Moore's *The Ballad of Baby Doe*. She was laugh-out-loud funny in *The Daughter of the Regiment*, the perfect minx in *Don Pasquale*, and terrific as the three heroines in *The Tales of Hoffmann*. She had powerful moments as Norma, but her pushing her voice was painful to listen to. One night after *Norma* at Ravinia in Chicago, we went backstage and I told Beverly the third and fourth acts were extraordinary. Without missing a beat, she asked, "And what was wrong with acts one and two?" Sometimes you just cannot win.

This is a wonderfully varied gallery of roles, but nothing compared to what she actually sang: seventy parts in 1,300 performances, including contemporary operas by Luigi Nono, Hugo Weisgall, and the aforementioned Douglas Moore.

I am convinced she would have been the greatest Mrs. Lovett in Stephen Sondheim's *Sweeney Todd* because of her comedic gifts and superb diction, which would have benefited Sondheim's challenging, complicated lyrics. She was a great singing actress.

As a person, she fooled most people into believing she was the sunny, funny, upbeat adorable redhead. But as Marilyn Horne is fond of saying, "They didn't see the dark side."

How could there not be a dark side given the challenges she faced with her children? But there was more: she was incredibly ambitious and, I think, bitterly resented how long it took for her to be recognized. After Cleopatra there was no holding her back. She sang endlessly and was game for anything. She'd fly in, do a performance, and fly out. She sang roles that interested her, her voice be damned. Once Cynthia invited her to lunch, then remembered she had a performance that evening. "I have to eat, don't I?" was her predictable response.

She will be remembered as an American phenomenon, despite her occasional forays abroad. She was a beautifully modulated singer with uncanny musical and theatrical instincts and modest vocal endowment. As she got older, a devastating combination of nature and her cruel abuse of her voice forced her to sing in a manner unworthy of her prodigious talent.

She will always be recalled fondly as Bubbles. The force of her irresistible personality prevailed during her career as it does today.

4
ON MY OWN

I cut my teeth on celebrity interviews at UPI, and all that exposure and experience helped me enormously when UPI suddenly closed down the Roto Service. They asked me to stay, even though they offered no specific job description. I decided to reject their offer and take the plunge to become an independent contractor, a plucky freelance writer.

My prime goal, my obsession, was to break into the *Arts & Leisure* section of the Sunday *New York Times*. That was where all my role models—Rex Reed, Tom Burke, Chris Chase—resided. These reporters not only got their subjects to open up and say outrageous things, their prose was piquant and flashy. Reed, for example, had Barbra Streisand "plotzing into a chair." Would that I could write like that!

In 1971 my dream came true. I wrote a painfully candid profile, on spec, of Julius Rudel, then the general manager of the New York City Opera. And Seymour Peck, the notoriously demanding editor of *Arts & Leisure*, the man who nurtured all my heroes, accepted it. I was in the door, 250 bucks a shot.

From that point on, it was pretty much smooth sailing. But I was ghettoized: only classical music. Peck knew he had a good thing going. He had finally found a reporter who could make classical music palatable to the masses.

My next assignment was Sir Georg Solti, just at the moment when he and his glorious Chicago Symphony were becoming superstars. After Solti was the superstar of them all, Luciano Pavarotti, and did we make music. The headline was "Pavarotti, Mama Mia," and suddenly the new guy on the classical beat was a writer in demand.

I coaxed the famously elusive Ronald Wilford, the powerful, cutthroat head of Columbia Artists Management, to sit down and put up with me for three hours. When the oddball piece was published, Wilford was livid and stopped talking to me for 30 years, after which a colleague of his made him revisit the piece and arranged a rapprochement lunch, which resulted in our becoming very close friends. I will admit it: I had a man crush on Ronald because I thought he was one of the most strategic, fearless businessmen I had ever met. I used to tease him and say I would take a leave to write his memoirs if I thought anybody would buy them. We were unlikely pals, until his death in 2015. I was asked to speak at his memorial, which thrilled me. It was a stellar affair: Marilyn Horne, James Taylor, Maurizio Pollini, Kathleen Battle, and Andre Previn, among many others, on the stage of the Richard Rodgers Theatre, whose tenant was *Hamilton* at the time. Peter Gelb, the Metropolitan Opera's general manager and a protégé of Wilford, also spoke: "I believe that Ronald would be pleased to be celebrated on the site of Broadway's new hit."

After Wilford, I did a roundup piece on rabid opera fans, surely a *sui generis* breed, the great Italian basso and heartthrob Cesare Siepi, the Met Opera's music director Rafael Kubelik, and the cocky Israeli fiddler/conductor Pinchas Zukerman.

There was range for sure, but I think what set these pieces apart was my fearlessness in asking often rude and aggressive questions. "Aren't you too short to sing *Tosca*, Ms. Scotto?" Also, for whatever reason, I seemed to be able to get subjects beyond their standard interview. Soon I began to develop a reputation as a troublemaker or, as one wag put it, "pushy Steve Rubin." That wag was a jealous competitor. What made me proudest was that I had joined the very exclusive club of "Peck's Bad Boys."

Working for Sy motivated me to get my subjects to delve into controversial realms. In all, over eight years, I wrote about sixty pieces for this unusually exacting and challenging editor. They covered the classical music waterfront: Birgit Nilsson, Montserrat Caballé (who bummed a half pack of cigarettes), Anna Moffo, Phyllis Curtin, Kiri te Kanawa, Carlo Bergonzi, Nicolai Gedda, Erich Leinsdorf, Colin Davis, Michael Tilson Thomas, James Levine, János Starker, Anthony Newman, Sarah Caldwell, Richard Tucker, Robert Merrill, Claudio Abbado, Sol Hurok, Lorin Maazel, and Zubin Mehta.

While working for Peck was mostly fun because he adored fomenters, there was one decidedly weird downside. Sy was rabidly homophobic and therefore ridiculously suspicious of any single man over 25. Worse, he drank the Kool-Aid of the *Times* to the point of lunacy. Once we were going over a piece about a popular singer when he asked me why I had omitted much of the well-known, overpublicized aspects of his career. "But Sy," I said, "they've been printed everywhere. All my stuff is new." "Stephen," he responded icily, "if it hasn't been in the *Times*, it hasn't been!"

Another time, we were preparing for my interview with a high-profile Broadway director, a rare non-classical bone thrown my way, and Sy asked me to ask him why he wasn't married. I didn't have the guts to do exactly that, but I did ask if he wanted to have a family. "Sure," he said. When Sy and I were editing the piece, he waspishly asked, "Why are you pushing the heterosexual angle, Stephen?" It was one of the very few occasions I lost my temper with him. "Dammit Sy, you asked me to ask him and that's what he said. Who cares anyway?"

The piece was put to bed. On a whim I rang up his press agent and asked if the director was gay. "Absolutely," came the reply. "Not in the pages of the *New York Times*," I said.

And then there was the tempestuous diva Renata Scotto, who masterfully employed the pages of the *New York Times* to renegotiate her contract with the Metropolitan Opera. She was surely one of the most expressive singers of her era, with a voice that could be acidic, wiry, and shrill when pushed beyond its essentially lyric limitations, but very beautiful in the appropriate repertory.

Scotto was a throwback to the "golden" days when sopranos took their divadom seriously. And she could be a handful when crossed. Artists like Scotto bring out the worst in me. I smell blood and become a shark. Aside from asking her if she was too short to sing *Tosca*, I once forced her to rate singers who are competitive with her:

Sutherland? "Great voice."

Freni? "Boring."

Callas? "Great actress."

Sills? "Great woman."

What a piece of work she was.

In the *Times* she made no bones about her diva status. "I sing for eight years at the Met now. And I don't have one new production, never, and no opening night either! I will not sing at the Met again until they give me a new production or opening night of some interesting opera for me and for the audience. For next year they offer me *Butterfly*. I don't want to sing *Butterfly*! I know the public. They like me and want me in something different, something new. All the Met say to me is compliments—*brava, stupenda, meravigliosa*, great success. Then they offer me *Butterfly*."

Scotto's bold frontal attack worked. She ultimately became a great favorite of music director James Levine and for a while was the Met's reigning diva. They even mounted Riccardo Zandonai's infrequently produced *Francesca da Rimini* for her. I have never encountered another artist who used the press in as overtly a self-serving manner as Scotto did and got away with it. And she could be fast on her feet too. To my query about being too short to sing *Tosca*, she snapped: "Is not *de* height *dat maka de* stature!" Score one for the diva.

Perhaps an even more tempestuous, considerably grander, and surely more generously endowed vocally diva, Leontyne Price was much more subtle in getting her way. No frontal attacks for her. You never really knew where you were with Price because, unlike Scotto, she kept her cards close. Without a doubt Price had one of the most beautiful voices I have ever heard. She produced a huge, golden sound that rolled over you like molten lava—big, luscious, and chocolatey, with gleaming high notes and a natural affinity for Verdi.

Voluble and almost shrill when she became emotional, Price, at least in 1973, often talked about race, "the monkey on my back." When she spoke about her family, particularly her mother, and her unfulfilled career at the Metropolitan, she abandoned her faux fancy accent that she often trotted out and became a true Southerner—she hailed from Laurel, Mississippi. Once, after a very long interview in her enchanting Federalist house in Greenwich Village, she walked me to the door and bid me adieux: "I am so sorry you cannot stay for tea and crumpets."

On another visit, she opened the door herself, and I was almost knocked over by a wall of sound. "I am so embarrassed, Stephen. I never listen to my own recordings, but this is a test pressing and I have no choice." I was embarrassed too because what she was singing was the Czardas from *Die Fledermaus*, hardly her natural repertory. "Leontyne," I said, at a loss for words, "who is conducting?" "Who cares!" was the tart response, and a perfect example of how funny she could be when she was being Leontyne instead of some fictional highfalutin diva.

Volatile, unpredictable, and ferociously emotional with me, I never knew what would set her off. "My career was simultaneous with the opening up of civil rights. Whenever there was any copy about me, what I was as an artist, what I had as ability, got shoveled under because all the attention was on racial connotations. I didn't have time to fight back as an artist except to be prepared and do my work and take that space because I was the only person allowed that opportunity. That is what it meant being black then. That is how much difference has been made in a decade."

She was right, of course. Marian Anderson was famously the first black singer at the Met. Then came Robert McFerrin, Price, and a hugely diverse group of wonderful singers: Mattiwilda Dobbs, Gloria Davy, Reri Grist, Kathleen Battle, Martina Arroyo, Grace Bumbry, Simon Estes, Shirley Verrett, George Shirley, and Jessye Norman.

"I can feel the difference, and it is so wonderful if you made the slight contribution to it," Price said. "That makes me feel just terrific, it means survival. It means you have had what it takes. And to have enough left to go on is fantastic. I am just not afraid anymore," Price exclaimed, her voice cracking with emotion. "I am not afraid to fail. And that makes things a lot better because when you are a token black, you can never allow yourself to even think in your subconscious that you can make a mistake. Talk to any black who has been in this particular palpitation and they will tell you the same thing."

I had to negotiate strenuously with Sy Peck to use the palpitation phrase. I told him, "It is a sublime example of the way she talks, and it is perfectly unambiguous." Happily, he agreed.

"You cannot afford not to burn the midnight oil longer than your colleagues, because in order to be heard, you have to be infinitely more prepared. So that if you get in the door, you have to accept and almost gobble up everything that comes with it. With it, in my case, was pressure. I didn't even have time to lose my temper and go through all the articles where wrong things were written.

"I think I am whatever normal means again. I think I am more professional, I'm growing up, I am becoming a woman. It has done wonders for me vocally. Maybe freedom is not being scared, and I am not scared anymore."

This extraordinarily honest and genuinely sincere outburst landed the Price profile on the front page of *Arts & Leisure*, no longer ghettoizing classical music to its own internal page deep into the section.

The singer I probably wrote more about other than Price was the charismatic heavyweight Luciano Pavarotti. I did two profiles for the *Times*, in *Arts & Leisure* and in the *New York Times Magazine*. But for sure the longest article I ever wrote about anything was a piece about The Big P, as Joan Sutherland called him, for a book called *The Tenors*, published in 1974, which also included portraits of Richard Tucker, Jon Vickers, Placido Domingo, and Franco Corelli. The book was put together by the PR man turned manager Herbert Breslin, one of the wiliest, most foulmouthed visionaries I have ever encountered. It was Breslin who masterminded Pavarotti's unparalleled ascent. Our paths would cross again many years later when I published Herbert's memoir of working with Luciano, *The King and I*, which turned into a controversial book because Herbert was completely comfortable being forthcoming about the kind of monster the tenor evolved into as his career grew considerably beyond opera.

But at the time I was writing about him, Luciano was undeniably an irresistibly flamboyant and endearing performer. He was in life as he was onstage—a natural. And if the world's a stage, Pavarotti was its biggest ham. He was always on, always up, Mediterranean to the core, which meant he was superstitious (finding a bent nail before a performance signified good luck), religious, and prodigious in his appetites, whether for food, fame, or *les femmes*. He was eons apart from the clichéd empty-headed tenor. He had common sense and native intelligence, all the traits that imply a lively, active mind, but not necessarily an intellectual one. His charm was easy, natural, and infectious. He was endlessly resourceful, shamelessly nervy and egocentric, yet appealingly childlike. In short, he was a spoiled brat. That he was lovable instead was a tribute to the monster-sized rascal, content in his corpulence, who gleefully thumbed his behemoth belly at the universe.

His singing was natural and unaffected, graceful, elegant, and very beautiful. Even though he could not read music, he was a well-grounded musician who phrased with finesse and landed on a note directly without employing scoops and slides to get there. Because he sang with such a natural ease, his diction was crisp and clean, and his pitch was dead-on centered. He felt music instinctively and his instincts were almost always correct. No whining, sobbing, belching, burping, or other typical "Italianate" traits reserved for country bumpkin tenors. The man had a Rolls-Royce voice and talent.

Together with the strategic Breslin, they created a career of legendary proportions. In the modern era he was surely the first operatic superstar tenor to engage in widespread solo recitals. "I go to the people who cannot come to me," the tenor said, which must not be interpreted as a charitable gesture. His first recital in America, in 1973, was in of all places Liberty, Missouri. Talk about out of town.

"I arrived in Kansas City and saw the bank Jesse James took the money from," Pavarotti recalled. "Then I stayed in the Presidential Suite, which had a piano Truman played on. Sixteen presidents slept there, and I have to tell you that the presidents of America must be very strong people because the bed

was so hard—God!—it was almost impossible to sleep." As for the concert
itself, "The college students didn't know me, but it was very beautiful."

After Liberty, he flew to Dallas, repeated the program, then had a 10-day
hiatus before Carnegie Hall and his New York recital debut. The concert was
completely sold out. In fact, a few days after the first newspaper announce-
ment of the event, Breslin received an unheard of $7,000 in checks and money
orders. There seems to be an underground mafia among vocal connoisseurs.
I remember being at Dimitri Hvorostovsky's New York recital debut at Alice
Tully Hall on March 4,1990. I have never seen so many tenors, conductors,
and other prominent people in classical music at one event. The same was
true of February 18, 1973, for the Pavarotti recital, the hottest ticket in town.

That none of the headlines the next day read, "Helen Morgan Returns in
Guise of Overweight Tenor," is a tribute to the sobriety of the classical music
press. To calm his obvious nerves and to give himself something to hold on
to, Pavarotti kept a giant white handkerchief in one or both hands throughout the concert. Actually, he must have gone through a box of them, such was
the twisting and mopping of sweaty brow and face that went on.

Pavarotti explained that he needed the mini security blanket because "at
a concert you must stay more still than is possible. The best way of not moving is to keep your hands together. But you can't do this if you are holding a
handkerchief. It's more natural this way and more practical. If I sweat, I can
use it too. I put a lot of Pierre Cardin cologne on it, so it smells beautiful too."
Talk about tenorial rationalizations.

Pavarotti could have come out in a straitjacket and the audience wouldn't
have cared. Within no time, the fever pitch built, and the screamers were
providing their own vocal storm. When New York audiences realize they are
in the presence of a truly great singer, they show their admiration appreciably.
The all-encompassing hysteria that reared its head at Carnegie Hall was just
further proof, if one needed it, that the Big P owned a brand of charisma and

spawned the kind of ferment that made Judy Garland concerts, including a historic one at Carnegie Hall, the unique events they were in terms of communication between soloist and listeners. I have often found the response of the audience as interesting as what was being performed onstage. At a starry New York Philharmonic concert version of Stephen Sondheim's "Follies," the audience was screaming and yelling rapturously from the moment the cast marched onstage.

Even the man himself was taken aback by the ferocious response. "I never saw anything like that just for me," he says. "I have seen a public like that in a beautiful opera performance, but it is for all the singers, not just for one. They touched me very much, molto. To make people behave like that, you have to do something. Music by itself is very good, but by itself it's not so important. It becomes important when it's doing something, going to somebody. When people scream like that, I can be sure I have done what is in my mind."

This sweet, almost simple-minded philosophy explained Pavarotti's mind-set perfectly. For all his antics and egomaniacal excesses, he was dead earnest about performing and took his responsibility very seriously. "Singers who cannot enjoy success are people who cannot enjoy life," he exclaimed. "There cannot exist a better job than ours. Working in art in general is the maximum thing. It's a profession because it gives you money, and it's an art because it gives you satisfaction. In the case of singers, the public, worldwide, gives us answers immediately. Painters have to wait a lifetime.

"I believe what I do, absolutely, no matter which role," he said. This sincerity, perhaps the first and foremost aspect of his art to travel across the footlights, was the essential ingredient of his mastery in not only holding the audience's attention, but in making it totally sympathetic to both Luciano Pavarotti and the character he was playing. The tenor was cognizant that he had this ability, but he could not define it. "I don't see me, so I cannot say. But I can tell you that Georg Solti came to see me backstage after *Daughter of the*

Regiment and said, 'Luciano, you can sing the telephone book, because when you come out you have something inside I cannot explain, but everybody is with you.' I cannot explain it either."

Maybe just as well. Pavarotti was hugely entertaining talking about the roles he liked and those he hated. He was very careful about choosing repertory, and not only because of vocal considerations. He wanted a showcase for his histrionic as well as vocal prowess. "I don't like to do *Traviata* because it is soprano's opera," he said. "The baritone comes out and sings a very beautiful duetto, then he has a fat aria and he gets all the applause. He is the second person of the night. Violetta is first. And Alfredo with his stupid character is last."

Faust was even more abhorrent to Pavarotti. "The more I see this opera onstage, the more I realize that this opera belongs first to Mefistofele, second to the lady, and third to the tenor. Faust's big aria, '*Salut! Demeure chaste et pure*,' is very incredibly boring!"

Pavarotti had misgivings about another vocally perfect part for him, the duke in *Rigoletto*, but here the problem was dramatic, and he seems to have mastered it. "The duke loves Gilda because she is a virgin, the Countess Ceprano because she is another man's wife, and Maddalena because she is a prostitute. The duke's a dirty Don Giovanni."

Whatever happened to the simple, charming, honest, and sincere man who voiced these sentiments as his career evolved into international megastardom? For one thing, his weight ballooned toward the end of his career to such a degree that he had to perform seated on a chair. I saw him once without a shirt, and it was truly horrifying. He looked like a beached white whale. He didn't seem to care that his hairpieces were ill-fitting and looked like they were colored with black shoe polish.

His behavior toward his wife, Adua, whom he married in 1961 and who bore him three daughters, was unconscionable. He had endless "secretaries," and he did very little to hide them. Finally, he married one of them, Nicoletta Mantovani, and had a daughter with her.

Worst of all, his erratic final performances lacked any of his expected magic. It was heartbreaking to hear a once-beloved artist perform so shabbily.

5

BORING AND BAD

After divas and divos like the tempestuous Renata, the voluble Leontyne, and the mischievous Luciano, there is a real challenge in interviewing dull, though well-meaning and sincere, artists. I remember the soprano Judith Blegen aspiring to be scintillating and even controversial and failing abysmally in both endeavors. The great Czech pianist Rudolf Firkusny was a lovely man but a dreary interview. The tenor Richard Tucker, in dead earnest, told me, "It's a lot of responsibility being the world's greatest tenor." He then pointed to my tape recorder and announced, "You can keep that for posterity, ya know."

Andre Kostelanetz, the ultimate purveyor of "light classics," took himself so seriously it became stultifying. He once told a colleague that, after working together for 20 years, he should be more relaxed and call him "Maestro."

Kostelanetz's archrival in the world of classics for dummies, Arthur Fiedler, music director of the Boston Pops, was another thing altogether, a crusty, cranky, and funny elder gent, who said that he loved to conduct genuine classical concerts because "every clown wants to play Hamlet." Fielder famously loved his booze and after a few nips became hugely entertaining.

Sy gave me a nifty plum when the great Russian composer Dimitri Shostakovich came to town. He also made me nuts by overpreparing me for the interview, and I turned in a piece that I am still ashamed of. Instead of dealing with the genius of a great composer, who was hounded and tortured by the Soviets, instead of being empathetic, I held a mirror up to his misfortune and reported on his tics unrelentingly. Worse, in a way, was the fact that Sy championed the wrongheaded approach.

The nasty letters to the editor confirmed my worst suspicions:

"Although expressing undeniable awe ('perhaps the world's greatest living composer'), and certainly presenting an affecting image of a great artist's physical presence, idiosyncratic psychic tensions, characteristic mannerisms and socio-esthetic attitudes, Stephen E. Rubin, in his interview with Dmitri Shostakovich, could not avoid assuming a tone for which the term 'snide' would hardly be an exaggeration."

Other than this unfortunate hiccup, Sy and I were a tremendous duo. I revered the editor because he motivated his talented team of writers to go for the jugular. Sy began to rely on me so regularly for articles, he floored me once with the unexpected offer of a full-time job. After a long period of intense soul searching, I turned him down. With hindsight, this was the best career decision I ever made. Had I accepted the offer, I would have been railroaded to a ghetto of sorts, underpaid and underutilized.

Such was my celebrity as a highly visible feature writer for the *Times*, I was offered a book contract. For an advance of $7,500, I cobbled together a collection of my opera pieces, added half a dozen new ones, and wrote a cocksure and controversial introduction (which Sy reprinted on the front page of *Arts & Leisure*), et voilà, I was a book writer. Despite all this attention, I have no idea how many copies *The New Met in Profile* sold, but I never received royalties and would guess it was in the very low four figures.

I cannot be upset about this paltry number because books by and about classical artists have never been big sellers. Of course, the exceptions are the superstars, Pavarotti, Domingo, Fleming, Norman. Beverly Sills's first memoir was a bestseller, her second, which I published, was a major disappointment. I was thrilled to publish Humphrey Burton's biography of Leonard Bernstein, but the sales did not reflect the quality and value of the book. The more experience I gained as a publisher, the more I avoided books I would have loved to publish but didn't because I knew they would not sell. At Doubleday I lured the great critic Peter G. Davis into writing a masterful book on American opera singers, and, despite its excellence, it underperformed. I tried a biography of Benjamin Britten at Holt, and it too sold very modestly. As much as I would love to publish music books, I learned to steer clear of them, having been burned too often.

To get out of the classical music rut, I begged Sy for assignments in pop, theater, and film. They were rarely forthcoming because Sy didn't want to distract the golden goose. I occasionally wrote for the *Times Magazine*, and while the pieces were mostly in classical music, I did get a chance to do a long profile of the pop singer Phoebe Snow that occasioned the only lawsuit I was ever involved in as a journalist.

I quoted the singer Janis Ian who said about Snow, "her record company and her manager and her lawyer all screwed her at once." What Janis actually said was "they fucked her over," which would never play in the *Times*. The manager sued Ian, the *Times* and me, and for the first time in my young career, I spent day after day with Wall Street lawyers. Ultimately, Ian got the case against her dismissed—her statement was protected opinion; we settled and the *Times* and I entered into a nominal agreement. What a waste of everybody's time and money.

The first piece I wrote for the *New York Times Magazine* got me banned from the New York Philharmonic. It was a profile of Pierre Boulez, then the hugely unpopular music director of the orchestra. I had a field day quoting Philharmonic players whining in unusual detail and vehemence about how dreadful it was to play under the modernist French maestro. The headline screamed "The Iceberg Conducteth," and that's all people remembered. They should have understood that writers do not write headlines, editors do.

My final piece for the magazine was of the great fiddler Isaac Stern, and the problems I had with the magazine over the experience are instructive, not only because of the cavalier and shoddy way the magazine treated freelance writers, but due to the culture of fear at the paper, especially between editors and senior management.

My editor Gerald Walker, author of the novel *Cruising*, which was made into a popular film starring Al Pacino, rang me to ask if I wanted to write a profile of Stern. Sure, I said. "I have to warn you," Gerry said, "that the idea came from Abe Rosenthal." Fine with me, I replied naively, I will get more space. Rosenthal was the much-feared, intrusive executive editor of the *Times*. If you think Sy drank the *Times* Kool-Aid, Abe brewed it.

I had a ball interviewing Stern and the "Kosher Nostra," his popular acolytes: Zubin Mehta, Pinchas Zukerman, Itzhak Perlman, and Daniel Barenboim. When I submitted the piece, Gerry called the very next day to say that the article was the best profile I had ever written for the magazine. First of all, I was floored by the swift response. The standard at the magazine was two weeks if you were lucky. And I was thrilled by his enthusiasm. I thought it was pretty nifty too.

When I heard nothing more, I called Gerry and asked what the hell was going on. "Ed thinks the piece is snide," he said. Ed Klein was the editor of the magazine then. He has since become a bestselling writer of bottom-feeding nonfiction. Klein was correct: the piece was snide, but ultimately it was a love letter to a man whose enthusiasms were as oversized as his body.

"So, Gerry, what are we going to do?" I asked.

"Ed wants you to come in so that we can all work on editing the piece together."

In I went, to a small, windowless conference room on West 43rd Street to confront Klein and the editors Dorothy Seiberling, Martin Arnold, and Gerry Walker.

It was four against one and an extremely unpleasant battle. We negotiated every sentence, and hours later a lively, saucy article became mild-mannered and toothless. If I had any backbone, I would have asked to have my name removed, but I didn't.

By mutual consent, the editors and I agreed that I would forgo my next assignment, on the novelist John Irving, and thus ended a brief career of eight articles for the *New York Times Magazine*, which I understand can still be a treacherous place for freelance writers.

6
WRITERS BLOC

The budding entrepreneur within me began to express himself when I came up with a scheme that was both daring and simple. Why not create a small collective of freelance writers, all of whom were pretty well known, and syndicate their articles to the individually edited Sunday roto magazine sections of large newspapers, none of which could begin to afford them singly? It seemed like a win-win proposition. The newspapers, many of which I knew from my UPI days, would be publishing high-caliber writers, and the writers would be paid multiply, thus making considerably more money than they did writing exclusively for one publication.

I approached a select number of my freelance buddies, and they were beguiled by the opportunity. I offered to run the fledgling operation out of my apartment, gratis. We called ourselves Writers Bloc (Cynthia's idea), and within no time we were off and running. We had a groaning board of options—celebrity profiles, science, business, pop culture, even a weekly column about the world of book publishing that set the stage for so much that would happen later in my career. Some of my colleagues included the brilliant former *New York Post* reporter Helen Dudar, who shared the publishing column with me and did occasional feature pieces; Ron Base, a terrific Canadian reporter and novelist; Richard Trubo, a lively California health and medicine reporter; and even some of the editors who bought our stuff.

Such was our success that a year turned into five years, and I was still running the operation gratis. It was a terrible conundrum. I was doing splendidly as a writer, but I felt guilty every time I took on an assignment because I felt I should be drumming up business for Writers Bloc. Conversely, when I was working for Writers Bloc, I felt the pressure of having to make a buck. After five years of this heady but exhausting schizoid existence, my sanity was definitely in question. I had splurged and hired a college kid as a part-time assistant, but I was still making daily trips to the bank and the post office. Where I got the energy, I honestly don't know.

I continued to write for Sy and many other publications, including *Ladies' Home Journal,* the *Saturday Review, Stereo Review,* and the *Psychoanalytical Review,* which assigned me a profile on Joanne Greenberg, who wrote *I Never Promised You a Rose Garden* under the pseudonym Hannah Green. For almost a year, I received many complimentary letters addressed to Dr. Rubin.

I used my non-*Times* assignments to steer away from classical music as much as possible and did a string of profiles of pop divas Helen Reddy, Carly Simon, and Janis Ian. I also interviewed some Hollywood royalty including Gregory Peck, Burt Lancaster (who was a huge opera fan), Michael Douglas, and Ryan O'Neal. One of my favorite pieces from that period was a profile of the shlock author V. C. Andrews, who was weirder than her novels. Andrews was confined to a wheelchair, and her mother, straight out of central casting, complained that the chair was tracking up the carpet.

Sometime in 1981 I received a consequential phone call from Richard Locke, the editor of the soon-to-be-revived *Vanity Fair,* asking me out to lunch. I did not know him and had no idea why he was calling, and I was even more confused after lunch. Locke tends toward being abstruse, and while we lunched regularly over a six-month period, I had no idea whatsoever he was going to offer me a job. Despite the fact that I found him mystifying, Locke was a perfectly agreeable fellow. I also was thrilled by the offer because at that moment the revival of *Vanity Fair* was the hottest ticket on the media forefront. Being a founding editor of the fabled magazine's revival was no small matter, nor was being able to join the ritzy playpen that was the great Condé Nast empire.

But I should have seen the writing on the wall when I was told in a classic Lockian miscalculation that all of us were going to be called "editors," which was needlessly confusing. To add further insult, we were housed in open-plan rabbit warrens, which was annoying. Locke had a plush giant office, and he had the powers build him a gorgeous desk that had an attachment to it so that all the knights of the round table could pay homage to the king. It was utterly ludicrous but nothing as compared to what lay in store for us poor minions.

It was indeed a playpen, at least at first. Unlimited expense accounts, vouchered cars, everything that Lauren Weisberger chronicled so brilliantly in *The Devil Wears Prada* (which I published years later). But once we started publishing, the more realistic staff members and media-savvy figures were mortified by the tight-assedness of the magazine, a perfect reflection of its editor in chief. The premiere issue was stillborn. On the cover was a dreary Milton Glaser illustration, a safe choice over other dazzling, audacious candidates. Inside was worse. The prime attraction, in its entirety, was Gabriel Garcia Marquez's novella *Chronicle of a Death Foretold*. That pretty much says everything you need to know. But the Debra Winger photo that looked like an ad for Wamsutta told the sad tale that the staff of *Vanity Fair* didn't have a clue.

There was talent galore: Elizabeth Pochoda, Patricia Towers, Moira Hodgson, Wayne Lawson, Carol Flake, and Walter Clemons, plus two stellar assistant editors, April Bernard and Don Guttenplan, and a host of extremely bright and appealing young assistants.

Here is how I solved the riddle of why these wonderful editors couldn't put out a decent magazine, even in spite of our detrimental leader. One Friday, a couple of months after we started publishing, I walked into Locke's office—he was in his bunker—closed the door because of his rampant paranoia, and confronted his entire desk and the round table, overflowing with piles and piles of unread proposals for articles. "Richard," I declared, "we have zero inventory. If we don't get some articles under way, we will not be able to put out the magazine." Pointing, I said, "I am taking your desk home for the weekend."

"What if there are personal notes in them?" he pathetically whined.

"You have half an hour," I responded.

When I walked in on Monday, I was a new man, considerably relieved that there were a huge number of terrific ideas for articles. I marched into Locke's office, again closing the door, and said, "Richard, we need to hire another editor. Not only do we have an empty cupboard, we are seriously understaffed." Much to my surprise, Locke seemed delighted by the idea and asked if I would undertake the initial search. I spoke to about twenty formidable candidates and chose a young editor from California. The only problem was she was going home, and Locke was on holiday. He graciously consented to come in to interview her the next day.

Afterward, he appeared at my rabbit warren, all smugness and good cheer. "I can well understand why you'd like her," he said of the editor, "but she has one major flaw: magazine experience."

"Come again?" I asked.

"Don't you realize," he said superciliously, all puffed up, "none of us has any magazine experience!"

Only someone as deluded as Locke could possibly think that the best way to put out a high-visibility, general-interest magazine was to staff it with neophytes in terms of magazine experience. It was the lame leading the blind. What a great disservice he did, both to his staff and to Condé Nast.

One time we really had to scramble to fill a hole in an upcoming issue. I turned to Walter Clemons, one of the dearest men and a stunning stylist, and asked him to plug the gap. Walter, like so many journalists, was better at fulfilling an assignment than at coming up with fresh ideas for articles. The best he could do was "My Journey to Discover Verdi," a viable endeavor for *Opera News*, but hardly the stuff that would appeal to readers of *Vanity Fair*, even in the most elegant Clemons prose. But we were literally stuck.

When it came time to lay out the piece, Alexander Liberman, Condé Nast's justly feared editorial director, decided he would do it, as opposed to our art director, Lloyd Ziff. Walter, Richard, and I joined Alex and his team of photo researchers in the art department, and the first words out of Alex's mouth were "this piece is so *bawring*." The blood drained from Walter's face. Walter was not only a perfect Southern gentleman but a diabetic as well, and fearful of his becoming physically ill, I forced him to leave the meeting.

When I returned, Liberman was at his most daunting. He had worked up a volcanic temper and was screaming at the researchers, "I want fat sopranos with hair under their arms, and fat tenors with bulging thighs, anything to give this *bawring* piece some *zest*." Three days later we reconvened, minus Walter, and it was electrifying to watch Liberman create anarchy out of a miasma of the ugliest photos I have ever seen of grotesque opera singers, and then slowly but surely with great relish transform the whole mess into order. The Russian émigré artist/photographer was undoubtedly a genius, but he was shockingly disrespectful and hurtful. For the second man in charge of Condé Nast to behave in this abusive manner was astounding to me. He was abhorrent.

I remember a much happier incident involving classical music when I assigned three critics to attend a screening of Hans-Jurgen Syberberg's avant-garde film of Wagner's *Parsifal*, all five hours of it. The reason for the multiple attendees was because I knew that Norman Mailer was a long shot to ever deliver a review. "What do I know about *Parsifal*?" he asked me when I phoned to invite him. "All the more reason to get your take," I told him.

He accepted and we sat next to each other. About two hours in, he excused himself. I panicked that he would never return. But he did. "Had you worried there, didn't I?" he teased when the film was over. "Just had to pee."

Mailer graciously and amusingly declined to review the film, which is what I expected, especially when we both were baffled to have discovered that the lead role was played by a boy and girl, although only sung by a tenor. I dealt with him a few times after *Vanity Fair* and always found him affable and rather jolly.

It soon became apparent that Locke's days were numbered. Unbeknownst to us, every time Si Newhouse, our owner, and Alex Liberman were behind closed doors with our deficient leader, they were beating him to a pulp. Poor Locke. Of course he was way too proud to share his misfortune with his staff because I guarantee we would have stood behind him.

Locke was unceremoniously sacked. I had the dubious honor of bringing his successor down from *Vogue* to meet his new, nervous staff. Leo Lerman, a popular bon vivant about town, who fittingly only wrote with purple pens, was seriously well past his sell-by date. But I am sure that Si and Alex, as creepy a duo as I have ever encountered, thought of Lerman as a short-term caretaker, because sitting in the bowels of *Vanity Fair* at that very moment was a dazzling firebrand from the United Kingdom named Tina Brown.

But first we had to deal with Lerman, whose antediluvian taste ran to black-and-white Irving Penn cover photos of Philip Roth and Susan Sontag. Very soon I realized that Lerman had no more use for me than I had for him. I was understandably perceived as of the old guard, and not necessarily shy about it. Lerman shut me out of everything and I was bored silly. Finally I marched myself up to human resources and said to the adroit Pamela Van

Zant, "We are wasting each other's time. I am not going to quit. Clearly you are not going to fire me." Her prompt response after checking with Lerman was that my assessment was correct. Condé Nast gave me a very generous kiss-off, and I joined the ranks of the unemployed.

Tina Brown and I had a long and successful association years later but our first meeting was considerably more cursory. During the short period when Lerman was editing *Vanity Fair*, I was summoned to Tina's closet-like office, told to close the door, and without any foreplay asked to "tell me everything." I had never laid eyes on this woman before and decided on the spur of the moment that discretion should be the order of the day. "You have got to be kidding," I responded and promptly left her office.

The next time we spoke, she was mightily restored to running *Vanity Fair* and called me at Bantam. "We made quite a mistake letting you go," she said. "Any chance you would consider returning?" Bad timing, I told her. I could not be happier where I am, thank you.

The life of an unemployed writer is a lonely pursuit. You sit around willing the phone to ring. When people feel sorry for your isolation, they take you to lunch and you indulge in an occasional alcoholic beverage. Big mistake. I often found myself being very unfriendly to my housemate, an adorable Lhasa apso named Brandy, late in the afternoon.

The entire *Vanity Fair* episode lasted 18 months. It was traumatic for me because I was appalled at how lackluster the magazine was. I made a pact with myself that, even if I had to start freelancing regularly again, I would never take another job unless I was sure it would be fulfilling. I loved my heady days writing for the *New York Times* and other publications.

I was invited to fly out to Los Angeles and rejected a sub editor position on the *Times*. "But we haven't discussed money," they said, clearly hoping that a Hollywood mind-set would win the day. No way. I flirted with the *Washington Post*, too, about becoming a cultural correspondent working from New York. But that came to naught.

So I accepted a couple of writing assignments. I kept reasonably busy, but being in a state of uncertainty is not ideal for a compulsive, anal person. And then like in every badly plotted novel, the phone rang again. It was Jack Romanos, the publisher of Bantam Books, inviting me to lunch.

7
NEOPHYTE PUBLISHER

I knew Jack from my Writers Bloc days when I coauthored their publishing column. He was one of my favorite sources because he loved to hear himself talk, and he was smart and entertaining, mouthing off sagely about publishing. Also, I was once present when an ugly personnel issue reared its head, and the fact that I never reported on it gave Romanos the security to trust me. We were good professional buddies.

Jack was 20 minutes late to the King Cole bar at the St. Regis, and without an apology he launched into an astute, indiscreet, and critical assessment of his publishing empire. *Why is he telling me this*, I wondered.

He said Bantam had no discernible profile within the industry and was definitely not aggressive enough about acquisitions. He suggested that since I knew everybody and was hardly shy or retiring, he wanted me to come on board as an executive editor. My prime responsibility would be finding books to reprint, which is a failsafe way to learn publishing because you have to "cover" all the major and minor houses.

I was flabbergasted. Good for you, Jack, for thinking outside the box. I accepted his offer to pursue this. Soon, I was dining with Linda Grey, Bantam's editor in chief, and we really hit it off. So I became an executive editor, and I got them up from $50,000 a year to $55,000. Much later, when it was clear how prescient Jack was and what a happy, productive duo Linda and I were, there was a general misperception that Linda was the "inside" person and I was the "outside" guy. This was disparaging to both of us. We did our jobs seamlessly and often traded inside/outside roles and, best of all, motivated each other consistently. We also had fun.

When Jack, very predictably, departed to become the publisher of Simon & Schuster nine months later, Linda and I really flowered. She was promoted to his role as publisher, and I gave her a list of candidates to interview for her job. Linda was unquestionably one of the most multitalented executives I have ever worked with, but she was dreadful at hiring people. After four months of torturing prospective candidates to say nothing of herself, she slumped into my office, defeated, closed the door, looked at me with beagle-sad eyes, and said, "It has to be you."

"Are you daft?" I responded. "I am nine months old and still learning the ropes of book publishing. I cannot have the added responsibility of a huge staff reporting to me."

"I promise I will help. I'll teach you. Don't worry." Linda was once an elementary school teacher.

We argued back and forth, and ultimately she prevailed. The guy who recently learned what a royalty was became the editor in chief of the formidable Bantam Books, with about twelve people reporting to him, all of whom had considerably more experience, including a couple of lalapalooza prima donnas. It was a classic trial by fire.

The most daunting challenge for me was a crusty, marvelous editor named Grace Bechtold. Grace, who was generally acknowledged as the doyenne of women paperback editors, acquired a nonstop stream of wildly diverse bestsellers including stars of the evangelical world Hal Lindsey and Og Mandino, Dr. Atkins, Raymond Moody, religious and inspirational books, even cookbooks. She was at Bantam for 40 years and hardly needed a green upstart like me telling her what to do. Here's how we reached a meeting of the minds.

She was in an auction for a book she desperately wanted. I told her to pursue a certain strategy, underbidding dramatically, which she found offensive. I insisted. When it worked, she cooed and giggled like a schoolgirl. I adored Grace because behind the leathery exterior and tough talk, she was a sweetheart. She also liked to booze it up, which endeared her to me even more.

In fact, at the Christian Booksellers Association, which we attended regularly, Bantam was the only company that had an open bar, thanks to Grace, who loved her martinis. Those good evangelicals started lining up half an hour before we opened our doors, and we literally had to throw them out at closing time. One night Hal Lindsey, who had a ferocious temper, did not approve of a fellow author, and we had to pull them apart before they started swinging at each other. Our journeys to the CBA were like extraterrestrial visitations. I adored my introduction to religious publishing via the evangelicals, for sure a harbinger of great things to come.

Another challenge was a very young editor who got loads of attention because of her work on Lee Iacocca's multimillion-copy bestseller. Nessa Rapoport began to believe in her own publicity. I was having none of it. Her antics have never worked with me. Also, all the terrific editors I have had the honor of working with always wanted to be in the background.

Among the others were Toni Burbank, a superb editor, who looked after Margaret Atwood and many others, and the wonderfully nutty Kate Miciak, a brilliant thriller editor. Peter Guzzardi, who acquired *A Brief History of Time*, was a standout on smart, often scientific nonfiction. When Peter showed me the editorial letter he wrote to Stephen Hawking, I had to admit that I couldn't understand most of it. We paid a modest $150,000 for Hawking's astounding book, which went on to sell millions of copies worldwide in good part because Stephen, who was irresistible in an almost childlike way, promoted it shamelessly.

Cynic that I am, I am convinced that the preponderance of people who bought the book never read it. I think most publishers will acknowledge that there are many books that are purchased more to display on one's coffee table than to read. This is true of fiction as well as nonfiction. Without a doubt, the greatest unread bestselling book of the last century was *The Name of the Rose* by Umberto Ecco. On the nonfiction front, Thomas Piketty's *Capital* is right up there. I honestly believe nobody much really read Thomas Pynchon books either.

Another person from those early days at Bantam who proved onerous was the legendary publisher Ian Ballantine, who was a consultant brought in by COO Alberto Vitale. Ian had an impish quality and a squeaky laugh but was not amusing when crossed. He had to get my approval before making an editorial acquisition, but he simply would not acknowledge the word *no*. After one of our heated conversations during which I rejected a project he wanted to buy, he would run off to Alberto's office. But I was considerably faster, got there first, and Alberto would have to referee a match between the icon and the neophyte.

In one of the weirdest contractual arrangements I have ever encountered, the cult novelist Tom Robbins had a clause in his deal with Bantam that guaranteed him three "editorial conferences" per year while he was writing a novel at a place of his choosing. Tom chose Two Bunch Palms, a spa outside of Palm Springs. When Tom's editor left, he asked if I could look after him because "Steve is an outlaw just like I am." Great praise from an aging hippie who played exclusively by his own rules, in his books as well as in his life.

"I am descended from a long line of preachers and policemen. Now, it's common knowledge that cops are congenital liars, and evangelists spend their lives telling fantastic tales in such a way as to convince otherwise rational people they're factual. So, I guess I come by my narrative inclinations naturally," Tom said. Those inclinations produced a wide-ranging group of novels all with fantastical titles including *Another Roadside Attraction*, *Even Cowgirls Get the Blues*, and *Still Life with Woodpecker*.

At Two Bunch Palms, Tom and his agent Phoebe Larmore (whose only other client was Margaret Atwood, whom Bantam published in paperback) would arrive first. Tom always brought along a different girlfriend, and Phoebe would book us massages, mud baths, and hot-tub excursions. Ninety-minute reading sessions were included in each day, after which we would discuss the pages we were given in sealed envelopes, which had to be returned afterward to the control-freak agent. It was an exercise in futility anyway since Tom would brook no editorial interference with his prose. But Tom and Phoebe pretended to enjoy hearing me and Matthew Shear, his publicist, engage in this faux literary tomfoolery. Nothing about this nonsense was mean-spirited; on the contrary, it was fun, especially if you like spas.

It was at Bantam that I got my first glimpse of corporate infighting. Our CEO, Lou Wolfe, was a mild-mannered former sales rep who loved the trappings of his job and lunched regularly at the Grill Room of the Four Seasons, where he indulged in two gin gimlets before each meal.

Every Wednesday at 2:30 we had a reprint meeting, a big deal at a mega paperback house like Bantam, which published countless numbers of books that needed to be kept in print. To watch the Machiavellian Vitale taunt the tipsy Wolfe was better than any Wednesday matinee on Broadway, especially if your taste ran to relishing a lion devouring a gazelle. I learned so much at those meetings, particularly about tricks of the trade, like removing expensive special effects, foil, or embossing from a jacket once the book was established. I also learned how to bulk up a book so we could charge more. Most important, I overcame the fear of a lot of publishers: up-pricing. I still believe that if readers want a book, they will pay for it.

Eventually Alberto maneuvered himself into Lou's job, which was hunky-dory until our pint-sized Italian-Jewish leader decamped to Random House.

Reeling, our German owners, Bertelsmann, installed Bernhard von Minckwitz as our interim CEO, a likable lightweight with no publishing experience of which I was aware. He was hopeless but nowhere near as dire as his successor, Paul Neuthaler, an academic, who became our new leader. Neuthaler's idea of management was very simple: if you take no chances, you won't make a mistake. To their credit, the Bertelsmann folks cut their losses and Neuthaler departed after nine abysmal months.

My biggest disaster occurred during this fallow period of bungling CEOs: a multimillion-dollar, three-book contract with the popular historical novelist John Jakes. Jakes was simply past his sell-by date.

Jack Hoeft, another former sales guy and an expert corporate gamesman, gave our owners a forthright proviso: make him the CEO, or he was out. They wisely bowed to his demand, and Hoeft prevailed as CEO until a smarter, definitely weirder combatant, Peter Olson, grabbed the reins out of his hands.

Once I got my bearings, I began to learn fast. Probably the most important lesson I grasped as a manager is that my staff came first. This may seem obvious, but not when you are in the throes of it. I have always said that the editor in chief's job is the toughest one in publishing because there is always somebody at your door, and often a very needy somebody. The great wag Michael Korda once put it perfectly: "If you are nice in this business, it lands in your briefcase for the weekend."

I grew up as a publishing professional during my six years at Bantam Books. I was the happiest guy around and it was reflected in my every endeavor. On the acquisition front, I was going gangbusters.

As paperback reprints I bought *The House of the Spirits*, *The Two Mrs. Grenvilles*, and, most significantly, because we worked together for the next 30 years, Pat Conroy's *The Prince of Tides*.

It all started on an airplane in 1985. I was finishing the final pages of *The Prince of Tides*, and the further I got, the more I became a public menace with my uncontrollable sobbing. Such was the emotional resonance of the book that made Pat a superstar. We ultimately paid a hefty price for the reprint rights, and one of our first moves was to book Pat as a breakfast speaker at what was then called the American Booksellers Convention. No one was prepared for the kind of manipulative and over-the-top performance Pat gave early that morning. The entire place was in tears, and they gave Pat a rousing standing ovation at the end. We Bantamites were beside ourselves because we realized a miracle had just occurred: a book had been "made" at an ABA. The hardcover was a major bestseller and our paperback was a blockbuster, helped considerably by a tie-in with the film, directed and starring Barbra Streisand.

For me personally, it marked the beginning of a dynamic journey Pat and I would take that extended for the next quarter of a century, first at Bantam and then at Doubleday, where he was published by Nan Talese. It was mostly a happy relationship because Pat was an appealing guy, much in the way a large, unkempt English sheepdog is.

But there were challenges. Pat's work habits were sloppy and unpredictable, fueled by bouts of alcoholism. He was underrepresented by a tony but inept agent, and until Marly Rusoff took over, he was shockingly underpaid. He was always short of money. Between his drinking, his unstable marital situation, and his cash flow issues, he was, to put it kindly, an adorable mess.

Once I had to babysit Pat at an American Publishers Convention in Florida where he was the keynote speaker. He was due to speak at 6 p.m., and I was sitting in my room getting more and more antsy. Finally the phone rang at 5:45. "We have a serious problem," Pat announced. "I forgot my shoes."

"What did you wear down here?"

"Sneakers."

"Did you remember to bring a tuxedo?"

"Yup."

"Okay, we'll start a new fashion trend, black tie and sneakers."

Over the years our relationship deepened, but never to an intimate degree. When I moved to England, I offered my apartment in New York to Pat, and he lived and wrote there. We saw each other in London too. But his deepest tie was to Nan, and they had what I can only characterize as the ultimate S&M relationship, with occasional flip-flopping role reversals, but mostly it was Pat as the dominant and Nan as the submissive.

This unhealthy state of affairs devastatingly erupted in 2009. I discovered how bad things were when Marly Rusoff, for whom I have the greatest respect and affection (she had been my first hire at Doubleday), visited me and related that Pat had worked himself into a fury about Nan, whom he thought treated him shabbily, especially about how long it took her to respond to his manuscript pages on the novel he was working on. Pat told Marly that he would not allow Nan to edit the book, which was, even Pat knew, bloated and in need of serious cutting.

In a move of unprecedented silliness, Pat hired a freelance editor at $20 an hour to give the book a haircut. Then his wife, Cassandra, a novelist herself, took a shot at it, and here they were, ready to submit it to Doubleday. But Pat was very clear: Nan could not lay a gloved finger on it.

When I read the book, I instantly understood that even by Conroyesque levels of untidiness, this was a mishmash of epic proportions.

I went into action, first visiting Nan and telling her the unvarnished tale of her author's lunacy. Despite her patina of ladylike breeding, Nan is tough as nails and a thorough professional. I think she was secretly bemused; she put up a brave front when I told her I would have to seek another editor, but that the book would be published by her eponymous imprint.

Then I went to see Phyllis Grann, the legendary publishing executive who had landed at Doubleday as the most unlikely senior editor in the business. Phyllis asked for this assignment—all she wanted to do was acquire and edit books. People fail to understand that as ruthless a corporate player as Phyllis was, she was an even more pugnacious editor. She read the 700-page doorstop overnight and told me how she would fix it. I thought it was a brilliant solution and rang Pat to ask if I could send Phyllis to South Carolina to visit him.

It was a disaster. Phyllis, in her unbridled enthusiasm to work with one of her favorite novelists, scared Pat to death. My next visit was to multitalented editor Gerald Howard.

"How would you like to edit Pat Conroy?"

"No, thanks. Way too sloppy for me."

I then stupidly called Pat and suggested some of my own edits. He was having none it. Although polite and friendly as always, he clearly was sick and tired of the whole muddle.

Finally, it came to me like a thunderbolt, and I called Christopher Pavone, now a bestselling novelist. When we published *Beach Music* at Doubleday, Chris was Pat's copy editor. They adored each other. So I sent Chris to Pat as a faux copy editor. His real job was to get Pat to make editorial changes and to cut the damn thing. By then, Nan told me she would lend a hand as well. Sub rosa, of course.

We eventually arrived at an imperfect manuscript that at least delivered a Pat Conroy experience, provided you read until the end. The rub was there was a ham-fisted subplot involving AIDS in the 1980s in San Francisco, but Pat would not hear of abandoning it.

We very carefully scheduled the book, making sure there was no one competing for the same reader, and Wendell Minor did his usual magic with a stunning, Conroyesque jacket. The first person I gave the manuscript to was Janet Cooke, our proactive sales liaison and mega Conroy fan. Janet called to sadly say she could not get through the book. "Bogged down in San Francisco, are you?" I asked her. When she said yes, I pleaded with her to finish it anyway. She did and agreed that once past the difficult subplot, the novel hummed along. Janet did her magic and talked the book up to sales reps and accounts.

When it was published in 2010, *South of Broad* debuted on the New York Times Best Sellers list at #1.

The first original novel I bought at Bantam was *Destiny* by Sally Beauman, a steamy, sexy potboiler for which we paid $1,015,000, then the highest advance ever for a first novel. It became a huge bestseller and, happily, earned out its advance. On the nonfiction front, I bought Patty Duke's memoir, *Call Me Anna*, which also climbed the bestseller lists.

Even then, in my salad days, I earned a reputation for rolling the dice and paying big bucks for books I thought had huge potential. We caused quite a storm when Bantam preempted Jorge Amado's *Showdown* for $250,000, the highest advance ever paid for a book in translation. Jealous competitors complained we were trying to buy respectability. Damn right.

I was barely a year old as a book-publishing professional, and I had already broken two records. For better or worse, my reputation for profligate spending continues to this day. Trying to publish big-ticket bestsellers is the riskiest game you can play. But it has been my modus operandi. Luckily, more of my crapshoots have worked than not.

Many times over the years, I was hugely relieved to come out of an auction as the underbidder. I pride myself on not allowing auction fever to infect me, but one can get carried away. Two of my most comforting losses are *Double Down*, successor to the runaway bestseller *Game Change*, which did not perform anywhere near as well as the first book, and a pair of novels by Gail Godwin, which lacked the bravura of *A Mother and Two Daughters*, Godwin's masterpiece.

Among examples of my most extreme overspending were books that became bestsellers but failed dramatically in terms of earning back gigantic advances or, worse, totally bombed. They include books by Carlos Ruiz Zafon, Billy Crystal, Mia Farrow, Simon Cowell, and Anita Hill.

In the winner's circle are books by George W. Bush, Rob Lowe, and Eric Clapton. Two of my greatest disappointments were losing a novel by Abraham Verghese to Nan Graham at Scribner, and the memoir of Robert M. Gates to Sonny Mehta at Knopf.

Figuring out what to spend for these books is a crapshoot. I do not care what scientific method you think will work—it won't. You sit and "do the numbers," try to predict how many copies a book will sell, but ultimately it's a shot in the dark, a spin of the roulette wheel. And you pray that you get more of these dodgy propositions right.

8
THE COCKY ROOSTER

Venerable corporate mascot Gertrude the Kangaroo brought Americans their first Pocket Book in her pouch in 1939. Ian Ballantine started an American outpost of England's indispensable Penguin Books in the same year. Avon Books was founded in 1941, Popular Library the year after, and Dell in 1943. But it wasn't until 1945 that the paperback revolution erupted when the cocky little rooster Bantam Books set up shop.

Their very first list, published on January 3, 1946, each book costing 25 cents, tells you everything you need to know about how savvy and prescient the Bantam folk were from day one. Talk about high-brow and low-brow!

Life on the Mississippi by Mark Twain
The Gift Horse by Frank Gruber
Nevada by Zane Grey
Evidence of Things Seen by Elizabeth Daly
Scaramouche by Rafael Sabatini
The Grapes of Wrath by John Steinbeck
The Great Gatsby by F. Scott Fitzgerald
Rogue Male by Geoffrey Household
South Moon Under by Marjorie Kinnan Rawlings
Wind, Sand and Stars by Antoine de Saint-Exupéry
The Last Time I Saw Paris by Elliot Paul

Then There Were Three by Geoffrey Homes

The Town Cried Murder by Leslie Ford

Mr. and Mrs. Cugat by Isabel Scott Rorick

Meet Me in St. Louis by Sally Benson

Seventeen by Booth Tarkington

What Makes Sammy Run? by Budd Schulberg

One More Spring by Robert Nathan

Oil for the Lamps of China by Alice Tisdale Hobart

Paperbacks in those days were considered shlocky and down-market. But this list speaks to a respect for quality that has always defined Bantam, even in its recent, much-diminished years. Its biggest hits were historic home runs, like 10 million copies of *Jaws*, and a splendid track record selling classics in the millions by Philip Roth, Truman Capote, J. D. Salinger, William Styron, Pat Conroy, John Steinbeck, Graham Greene, Ray Bradbury, and John Hersey.

Bantam evolved slowly, but it wasn't until Oscar Dystel joined the company in 1954 that it became the progressive company that I joined. A Harvard Business School graduate, Dystel wrote his thesis on "Paid and Controlled Circulation in the Business Paper Field," which earned him a reputation as a sharp businessman. This fascinating period in Bantam's evolution is wonderfully chronicled in Clarence Petersen's *The Bantam Story*, which astutely studies paperback publishing in its entirety, not just Bantam. Once Dystel joined the company, he immediately isolated ten problems confronting the fledgling company, most seriously too many books printed, distributed, and returned unsold.

"Nobody knew who was selling to whom or for what reason," Dystel told Petersen. "We were operating on a principle, industry-wide, that I thought was appalling. It was like an army sending out 1,000 soldiers and getting

900 killed to capture an objective. We were flooding the market to sell one hundred copies, and those returns were killing us. We were losing hundreds of thousands of dollars."

Dystel's diagnosis for curing the ailing business came quickly. "The first step was a tremendous cut in wholesaler inventories and the institution of a level inventory plan among wholesalers. In 10 months we reduced the inventories in wholesalers' warehouses from 6.9 million to 4.8 million books.

"The next step was a more realistic attitude toward initial print orders, keeping in mind conditions in the marketplace and the sales expectancy per title, and remembering the good psychological effect on the wholesaler of keeping a title slightly under-distributed initially. The first printing would be conservative; even though a title could have a big potential sale, we would concentrate on reorders."

Dystel also addressed the diversity of the list, which, at the time he joined, had far too many westerns. He quickly understood the value of having a strong backlist, which are titles that sell way beyond their initial release. He also knew that sometimes you have to invest money to earn money. In those days paperback advances were in the neighborhood of $2,000. His first gamble was $25,000 for *Battle Cry* by Leon Uris, which became a multimillion-copy bestseller, a successful film, and established a long association with the author that lasted until his death.

When no hardcover publisher was interested in William Peter Blatty's *The Exorcist*, Dystel bought both hardcover and paperback rights in 1971. He later sold the hardcover rights to Harper & Row. The rest, as they say, is history. Bantam sold millions of copies, helped, of course, by the hugely popular film.

In those exhilarating days, hardcover houses without paperback affiliations sold paperback rights to their big sellers. Bantam shelled out $350,000 for Philip Roth's *Portnoy's Complaint*, a genuine bargain. When Dystel read

The Valley of the Dolls by Jacqueline Susann, he instantly scooped up the paperback rights before the book was published. It became the fastest-selling paperback in history at that time, with a 4-million-copy first printing in July of 1967 and another 4 million copies by the end of the year. There was no denying Dystel's unerring expertise in discovering novels that defined what the booming mass-market paperbacks eventually became.

Soon hardcover houses woke up to the reality that they didn't need to pay paperback houses royalties if they published the paperbacks themselves. This may seem alarmingly obvious, but it wasn't at the time because the boundaries were ridiculously strict. But paperbackers, always more agile than their hardcover counterparts, began creating their own hardcover companies to feed their mass-market lines. Bantam, always ahead of the crowd, went one step further: they bankrolled expensive acquisitions for cash-strapped houses, most notably Tom Wolfe for Farrar, Straus & Giroux and Judith Krantz for Crown Publishers.

But all wasn't well in paradise.

This was the period when Bantam revolutionized the industry by publishing a string of mass-market hardcovers that sold in numbers nobody had ever achieved in hardcovers. Bantam was earning massive profits. I remember giving members of my staff 20 percent salary increases, more than double the norm.

One day Linda Grey and I had a sobering meeting with our CEO, Alberto Vitale, that taught me a lesson I have never forgotten. We looked at profit and loss statements that did not include our hardcover mega successes. We were in serious trouble. In our enthusiasm to impress the industry that we were true hardcover publishers, not mere reprinters, we had begun to ignore what kept the formidable engine room of this dynamic company afloat: the mass-market paperbacks. Luckily, thanks to Vitale, we discovered the cancer early and set about battling the disease immediately, but it was really scary there for a moment. To this day I always say, the minute you take your eye off the ball, you get into trouble.

The clout of the mighty Bantam machine is best demonstrated by how the company published instant books. I will never forget when we published an instant book on *The Tower Commission Report*. I received a call from my friend Jonathan Segal, then at the *New York Times*, who wanted to copublish the report with us. The *Times* would supply an introduction by the popular R. W. Apple, and we would produce and ship the book.

We created a war room—I have never seen a company mobilize so magnificently. The report was released on a Tuesday, and I had a finished book plus press release by Thursday. We were in 90 percent distribution on Friday. Ultimately, the $5.50 book netted in excess of half a million copies.

Bantam had about seventy of these "instant books" since it began the program with the *Report of the Warren Commission on the Assassination of President Kennedy* in 1964. It sold 1.5 million copies and was acknowledged as a bold and inventive publishing feat. The 800-page tome was on sale within 80 hours after it was released to the public.

I was blessed to have started my publishing career at Bantam, not only because it was the gold standard, but because it was steeped in the most progressive way of publishing paperbacks, never mind the brief hiccup with our hardcover fixation. The can-do attitude there was awesome.

People forget how many of the most revolutionary and successful publishers in the industry got their start in paperbacks: Peter Mayer, Sonny Mehta, Susan Kennedy Peterson, Carole Baron, and Phyllis Grann come immediately to mind.

Not only was I grounded in the process by having to cover a huge number of publishers for reprints, I also learned early on that there is a great land out there west of the Hudson, and the readers who live there love and buy books. Not necessarily the books championed by high-end publishers, but a rich combination of everything from Louis L'Amour to William Styron, just to mention two of Bantam's biggest bestsellers.

My incomparable six years at Bantam, working with talented colleagues like Linda Grey, Alberto Vitale, Stuart and Irwin Applebaum, and Grace Bechtold gave me, novice that I may have been compared to them, the conviction and fortitude to undertake my next assignment.

9
DOUBLEDAY

It had been four years since Bertelsmann bought Doubleday in 1986 for $485 million. The Germans and Vitale made the bold decision to install Nancy Evans as president. Nancy, although a popular executive, came from the Book of the Month Club, and had zero experience in publishing original books. Book clubs choose their selections from finished manuscripts that had usually been edited and were already destined for publication, as opposed to publishers who buy books in various early stages of development.

Word was out that Doubleday was floundering under Nancy's leadership. Financially, rumor had it the company lost $6 million on a turnover of $60 million. I harbored secret, unformed fantasies of taking over the troubled company, but no one was more shocked than I was when the Bertelsmann management actually offered it to me.

It was wrenching leaving Linda and my colleagues at Bantam. But there was no way I wasn't going to face what would surely be the greatest challenge of my career thus far. I was so naive. I didn't have a clue what was in store for me and how troubled the almost century-old Doubleday was, to say nothing of the draconian measures I would have to take to bring it back to fiscal and publishing health.

In January 1990, when I became president and publisher, Doubleday was publishing 465 books a year. That was the tip of the iceberg. Star authors had their own American Express cards: we put a stop to that immediately. The florist bills could easily have supported a small third-world nation. But most distressing was that every time you picked up a rock at Doubleday, something slithered out from underneath that you didn't even know existed.

Publishing in excess of 400 books annually, including a juvenile division, was pure folly. To get a proper sense of perspective, most traditional hardcover publishers at that time were barely shipping more than sixty books annually. In my lexicon, being a "generalist" publisher, which Doubleday was then, meant that you were an "unfocused" publisher. There is simply no way of concentrating on marketing that many books. Worse, how many publishers have the expertise to serve a groaning board of fiction, nonfiction, religion, business, illustrated, juvenile, health and fitness, and lifestyle books?

Believe it or not, Doubleday published that ridiculous number of books to keep the printing presses they owned busy. But those days were long gone, so we decided that first, we would shuck illustrated books, generally bought as finished books from packagers. Next I had to address the problem of returns. The company would purchase 20,000 books, ship 12,000, and get 6,000 returned, which meant that of the 20,000 only 6,000 sold—not a fiscally sound way to operate.

Eventually, we turned over the entire juvenile division to our colleagues at Bantam Doubleday Dell, our parent company then. We decided to concentrate on popular and literary fiction, narrative, celebrity and biographical nonfiction, business, and religious books. In all, 200 books a year, a drastic cut of more than 50 percent from what Doubleday had been publishing.

To accommodate staffing to that reduced number of books meant that we had to relieve a number of editors of their jobs. We adapted a very slow process of sacking people, in the most humane fashion, with rich financial packages. There was literally no fallout from what we were doing, until Leon Uris, a longtime Doubleday (and Bantam) author, most famously of *Exodus*, got wind of the fact that his former secretary was being let go, and he went public with the news in *Crain's New York*.

This was entirely my fault. I knew Lee from my days at Bantam and thoroughly objected to his egomaniacal, loudmouthed behavior. Instead of behaving professionally myself and calling him when I arrived at Doubleday, I chose to ignore him, and he was understandably incensed. We finally had it out on the phone when he asked me in no uncertain terms, "Just who the fuck do you think you are?" He was completely justified and I ate a giant portion of humble pie.

Another name-brand author I had difficulty with was Gay Talese, journalist and book writer extraordinaire, who was married to Nan Talese, who had her eponymous imprint at Doubleday. This problem was much more subtle and riddled with all kinds of emotional baggage.

Nan and I had a rocky start when I came to Doubleday because she wanted to report to Peter Olson, but she and I eventually came to a meeting of minds and evolved into a great team. I adore and respect Nan.

Gay was another matter altogether. He announced to me that he would take his $5 million multi-book contract elsewhere because he could not write for a corporation that employed his wife. This was pure rubbish.

I think both Taleses were very wary of a "paperback publisher" guiding their destinies. Very much in retrospect, I can well understand their hesitation. I had six years of experience as a publishing professional at a mass-market house that only reprinted works of literary merit, but rarely initiated them. I may have talked a good game, and personally much preferred reading the high-minded books, but they weren't wrong. Proof came soon enough. Nan wanted to partake in the auction for Philip Roth's *Sabbath's Theater*. I read it and told her in no uncertain terms she could not even attempt to buy it. Of course, I was gravely mistaken.

I visited Gay in his bunker, which is how the couple refers to his working quarters in their posh Upper East Side brownstone. He was friendly, polite, and resolute: he was moving on. I was terribly upset to lose such a significant writer. Gay has always been a hero to me. It was when I read his famed *Esquire* profile, "Frank Sinatra Has a Cold," that I decided journalism was the career path I wanted to pursue. Years later I reread all his pieces, which were collected in a book, and was stunned at how well they all held up. Sadly, in retrospect, I dodged a bullet by losing Gay. Predictably, he went to Knopf, always perceived as more upscale, but where his books never sold at the level they paid him.

Between the very slow pace of firings, one or two editors got a sense of the lay of the land and resigned, and we were soon at the correct number of staff. After all that unfortunate negative energy, we could finally begin the daunting challenge of rebuilding a once-great publishing house.

During the early years of the twentieth century, west of the Hudson, Doubleday was always a brand with instant recognition. Founded in 1897, it was very soon publishing bestsellers by Rudyard Kipling, Bram Stoker, Joseph Conrad, and Booker T. Washington. As Doubleday and the century grew together, that list broadened to include Helen Keller, Andrew Carnegie, Upton Sinclair, Sigmund Freud, O. Henry, Somerset Maugham, Aldous Huxley, Sinclair Lewis, Daphne du Maurier, Herman Wouk, Stephen King, Alex Haley, Isaac Asimov, Bill Cosby, Michael Jackson, Bill Moyers, Margaret Atwood, Ian McEwan, Pat Conroy, John Grisham, and Dan Brown.

Doubleday has published seven American presidents, two vice presidents who eventually made it to the White House, and seventeen Pulitzer Prize winners. Of its Nobel laureates, Rudyard Kipling was the first Englishman to win the prize, Selma Lagerlof the first woman, Sinclair Lewis the first American, and Naguib Mahfouz the first Egyptian.

It is surely an illustrious and impressive array of diverse authors. But when I arrived in 1990, Doubleday was perceived as the *Titanic* about to go under. During the fiscal year 1989–1990, manufacturing costs, which include the prices of paper, printing, and binding, rose to a stratospheric 48 percent of sales. In a good year, manufacturing cost is around 15 or 16 percent. This soaring overhead cost was due to a deadly combination of overspending on fancy effects, low printings, and high returns.

Of course, cost cutting was first on my agenda. Nancy Evans, understandably, was appalled by the way Doubleday books looked when she arrived. They generally were printed on toilet paper and had jackets that were produced on the cheap. Nancy had impeccable taste, but her improvements helped production costs to skyrocket. To further complicate the financial situation, Nancy fell prey to the oldest game in the book: overpaying for projects to prove that she and her company were players. This meant that in addition to the production costs, write-offs were astronomical.

But once we were able to get staffing, production costs, and write-offs under control, we could then focus on getting a team together to publish the best books possible, in a financially responsible way.

The person who helped me most in envisioning what Doubleday could be under a new regime was a stalwart from the old regime, William G. Barry, who had joined Doubleday in 1979. Being a Jesuit by training, Bill could complicate a paper napkin, but he was also a humane pragmatist who offered invaluable counsel about who should and who should not be part of the new team. Bill was a crackerjack businessman with intimate knowledge of back-office operations, hardly my area of expertise in those days, and he helped tremendously to stop all the money Doubleday was hemorrhaging.

Best of all, Bill was a fair, kind, upstanding guy with an affable personality and an ingrained savviness about the publishing business. We were a terrific balancing act.

Bill was very close to our superstar editor, Jacqueline Onassis, who was the only one I knew who ever called him Billy. What was it like being Jackie's boss? Curious, to put it mildly, but gratifying as well.

The greatest misperception about Jackie was that her being an editor was something of a lark. Wrong—she was dead earnest about her job. She came in three days a week and was deeply committed to producing beautiful-looking books of great endurance. She adored her authors, who returned her affection unreservedly. The composer/conductor Andre Previn offered an insightful tribute in a book we published celebrating Jackie by her authors: "Her ideas were always seemingly indirect, but upon closer examination absolutely practical and useful. She had an unbeatable sense of humor and we laughed a great deal. Her faith in the project, as indeed all of her projects, was absolute, and I cannot imagine anyone not being the better for having worked with her."

Much to my surprise, Jackie loved undertakings that earned money. If I told her a book she was supporting would have a negative financial prospect, she backed away immediately. But if she was enthusiastic about a potential project, she could, like any good senior editor, become stubborn and fierce-willed. I can remember countless times when I would find her waiting patiently outside my office for a meeting to end so that she would get my attention first on a much-desired project.

Surprisingly, she could also be very insecure. We once were scheduled to have a conference call with the formidable Maya Angelou, and as we were preparing for it, Jackie suddenly demanded that I "ask all the tough questions." Why? I responded. "She scares me," Jackie said forthrightly. "Maybe you scare her," I said. "No way," Jackie said in her signature whispery, campy, unmistakable voice.

Jackie was an undeniably potent weapon in Doubleday's weak arsenal. Who wouldn't return a phone call from one of the world's most prominent women? But Jackie never played this trump card in the office. On the contrary, she was modest and unassuming, wearing her customary trousers and blouse, and occupying a small, tacky office, purposely situated as far as possible from reception to avoid the gawkers. She usually brought in cut-up celery and carrots wrapped in tinfoil to munch on. She hated going out to lunch because no matter where she went, she created a frenzy or, worse, there were paparazzi.

CEOs do have their perks, and our leader then, Jack Hoeft, insisted on having lunch with his most famous employee. After breaking the bad news to Jackie, I called a quiet, French restaurant we often frequented, informed them I was bringing in Mrs. Onassis, and warned them that if they treated her any differently than any other customer, I would never allow Doubleday personnel to eat there again. When she entered the tiny restaurant, it seemed as if all the guests held their collective breaths. But other than that and a boring lunch, it was a very uneventful encounter.

Speaking of her creating a form of delirium, Bill Barry tells an anecdote that is not only hugely entertaining but also is evidence of her wicked sense of humor. The two colleagues were flying to Washington to try to lure in a senator's book, and they arrived very late for a 4 p.m. shuttle. There were only two seats left on the jammed plane, and they were all the way in the back. Jackie caused virtual pandemonium when she marched down the aisle of the bustling aircraft. When they were finally seated, Jackie turned to her companion and said, "Oh Bill, *everybody* knows you!"

The other celebrity in the office was Jackie's secretary, Nancy Tuckerman, a marvelously crusty, no-nonsense woman who wasn't in the least impressed by her boss. "Tuckie" was a hoot and reveled in telling stories about her legendary honcho, like the time she took her to the company cafeteria for lunch. Once seated, Jackie jumped up to get an iced tea, which she failed to pay for. "I could see the *New York Post* headline," Tuckerman smiled, "Onassis Arrested for Nonpayment." It gets better. When they were ready to leave,

Nancy explained that they had to deposit their trays in a designated area. Jackie loved the new experience. "It's like going to the dry cleaners," she exclaimed. "Yeah right," Nancy said to me, "when was the last time she was in a dry cleaners?"

Another time, Nancy arrived in my office fresh from a nifty face-lift. She looked exactly like herself, only 10 years younger. What did Jackie say, I asked. "She has chosen not to notice," was Nancy's tart response. Despite her fondness for having fun at the expense of her stellar boss, Nancy was dedicated, fiercely loyal, and very fond of Jackie.

Strangely, there was something about Jackie that made all of us not only like her but want to protect her. Was it vulnerability? Maybe. But there was a standard rule at Doubleday that I insisted be rigorously observed. We never spoke of her publicly and we never, ever published anything about her or the Kennedy family. Except once.

Among the many burdens I inherited at Doubleday was a long-standing arrangement to copublish books with *Spy* magazine. The most successful of this series was the hugely popular *Separated at Birth*, but most of the paperback originals were sophomoric and modest sellers. One of the worst was a faux yearbook called *Spy High*.

One day our managing editor marched into my office, looking like her family had been decimated in an automobile accident, and said, "Jackie is in *Spy High*." I couldn't believe my ears. I called the editor, Paul Bresnick, and asked what the hell was going on with putting a mean-spirited Jackie roast in that silly *Spy High*. "It was a judgment call," Bresnick said defensively. A stupid one, I responded.

I gathered my wits about me, rang Mrs. Onassis, and asked her to join me in my office. "Oh, this is serious," Jackie said, taking a look at my face. I explained that Bresnick had let the *Spy* pranksters put her in their alleged humor book, and it was a nasty piece of work. "Do you want to see it?" I asked her. Jackie put up her hands protectively as if to say "Spare me!"

"Here's what we can do," I explained to her. "Since the offensive feature is an entire signature," which are a group of pages to be worked into the binding as a unit, "I can have it excised entirely. The downside to that is, who knows what the *Spy* people might do. They could go public and cause an embarrassing ruckus for you. In all candor I should also tell you there are other insulting potshots taken at members of your family.

"How do you want me to proceed?"

"Get me out and let the rest of my family fend for themselves," was Jackie's unforgettable response. I do not think I ever liked her more. She was the most ladylike killer survivor I had ever met. Ironically, despite all our worrying, we never heard a peep from *Spy*.

When Jackie was diagnosed with non-Hodgkin's lymphoma, she came to tell me. I have rarely heard devastating news delivered with less self-pity. Valiantly, she tried to come into the office during her chemotherapy treatments; she looked ravaged and, shocking for her, her wigs were often askew. It was dispiriting.

When she finally succumbed, there were tears everywhere. The night before her funeral, Bill and I went to prayers in her mammoth, elegant Fifth Avenue apartment. The sight of Carolyn and John was enough to break your heart. The celebrities were wall-to-wall. At one point Ethel Kennedy came in followed in single file by all her children in age descending order. It was like watching an errant gene gone rampant.

The next morning was the funeral, at St. Ignatius Loyola Roman Catholic Church, on Park Avenue and 84th Street, where Jackie was baptized as an infant and confirmed as a teenager. It is a very beautiful, old neoclassic limestone church, and it was filled again with celebrities and family. Maurice Tempelsman, her companion at that time, whom I think Jackie loved (I teased her that Jewish guys make great husbands), and who was very depressed after her death, read a poem. Director Mike Nichols, a very close friend, read scripture, and Jessye Norman sang Franck and Schubert gloriously. All her close relatives spoke as well. I cried nonstop.

The next day I went into overdrive. For the first time, I went public about my deep admiration for Jackie and did a round of about forty TV, radio, and print interviews in two days. It was exhausting but so gratifying to finally reveal to the world how absolutely terrific she was as a colleague and a person.

In honor of our distinguished colleague, Doubleday published two exquisitely printed small books, with cases in her favorite "Onassis blue." One contained short tributes to their editor by her writers, and the other reprinted the entire funeral service.

Jackie's oeuvre as an editor reflected her wide-ranging interests. There were the expected bestsellers—*Moonwalk* by Michael Jackson, children's books by Carly Simon, and *Dancing on My Grave* by Gelsey Kirkland. There was also the most extraordinary combination of high-end fiction and non-fiction by an incredible roster of authors, including Naguib Mahfouz, Ruth Prawer Jhabvala, Louis Auchincloss, and Dorothy West, plus Bill Moyers, Jonathan Cott, Andre Previn, Diana Vreeland, Edvard Radzinsky, George Plimpton, Martha Graham, Judith Jamison, and Olivier Bernier.

I once asked Jackie how she had such a discriminating nose in choosing books of quality that also sold well. "I am only moved by books that interest me," was her typically restrained reply.

Let's let George Plimpton have the last word on this unique woman. Like Andre Previn's, this was written for the book we published about Jackie as an editor:

"I think one of the curious pleasures of doing a book with Jackie was that one felt part of a conspiracy—that somehow she had infiltrated into enemy territory and was there to guide her writers through the barbed wire and across the trenches. The editorial relationship was very personal. Her voice over the telephone was certainly conspiratorial: 'I am going to get you more money, but don't tell anyone!'"

My first three hires at Doubleday had not worked out very well—Marly Rusoff was a terrific director of publicity, but once we gave her marketing as well, things began to go awry. Susan Moldow was a skilled editor in chief, but she only lasted a year before she went to work for her husband, William Shinker, at HarperCollins. The brilliant Ann Godoff lasted less than one month as executive editor before she returned to Grove Atlantic in an elevated position.

With Susan's departure, I promoted senior editor David Gernert to the top editorial post, and it turned out to be a momentous appointment on many levels. David was a creature of Doubleday, having started as a young lad in the subsidiary rights department. He worked his way up to senior editor, making some sensational acquisitions including *A Shot in the Heart* by Mikal Gilmore and an unknown novelist named John Grisham. Eventually, David would leave Doubleday to become John's agent and to build himself one of the happiest, most successful agencies in the business, the Gernert Company. He also became one of my closest professional friends. David, who resides mostly on Planet Gernert, is a kindhearted, generous, compassionate boss, a scrupulously honest and forthright agent, and the best drinking buddy a guy could have.

The Firm, the first Grisham novel David bought, was scheduled to be published in March 1991, two months after I arrived at Doubleday. While

I was still at Bantam, we were sent *The Firm* as well. It was submitted to our thriller editor, who rejected it, which I didn't know until the book took off. Susan and I read it as soon as we were in place, and we were completely bowled over by its page-turning energy. We had ordered a 25,000-copy first printing, not shabby at all for a book by an unknown. We were determined to market *The Firm* to lawyers, whom we felt would be the core readers for it. We succeeded beyond our wildest expectations.

Publishing *The Firm* was exactly what was needed at that point: a potent shot in the arm for the depleted Doubleday morale. I thought I had had a lot of experience with successful books at Bantam, but nothing prepared me for the word-of-mouth sensation *The Firm* exploded into. Since all we ever did with the propulsive bestseller was reprint, *The Firm* has a scrupulously clean sales history. Not bad for a novel by an unknown writer.

Not for long. John Grisham soon became a household name. We capitalized on John's good looks and plastered his handsome face in all our ads. John hated being a poster boy—he even went through a period when he was purposely photographed unshaven—but he went along with all the promotion. Remember, this was a guy whose first novel, *A Time to Kill*, was turned down by most mainstream publishers but eventually was picked by Wynwood Press, which nobody had ever heard of. Eventually, Doubleday purchased the copyright to John's first and favorite novel. Then we published a hardcover edition of *A Time to Kill*, and it became a huge bestseller. At that point you could put John Grisham's name on the phone book and it would sell.

John is the ultimate pro, at first delivering a book a year like clockwork, then two and sometimes three. And he started a very successful juvenile series, the Theodore Boone kid lawyer books. John, much like his friend Stephen King, is a natural-born storyteller. I used to tease him regularly: "John, you have a disease. It's called 'writing.'"

The reason John's output is so spectacularly prolific is because he always has two or three stories simmering on the back burners of his unusually fertile mind. Despite his detractors to the contrary, they are all different. Yes, they may all be legal thrillers, a genre one could say he brought to sublime fruition, but they are thematically eons apart. How many "thriller" writers can claim to have written novels about cotton farming (*A Painted House*, his most autobiographical book), football (*Playing for Pizza*, which to my surprise and delight was dedicated to me), college basketball (*Bleachers*), the commercialization of religious holidays (the wildly successful *Skipping Christmas*), and one masterful work of nonfiction (*The Innocent Man*). I have begged John to return again to nonfiction, but he resolutely refused. "It's just easier to make it all up," he says.

Not that one could ever call John lazy. In 2018 he surely shocked me and I am sure a good portion of his giant fan base by producing a novel that required the kind of research very few authors would undertake at that stage of his career. *The Reckoning*, in its awesome ambition, reminded me of Philip Roth's *The Plot Against America*, an unexpected work of alternative history published in 2004 that required huge amounts of groundwork.

The Reckoning opens with a shocking admission. Pete Banning, our hero, tells us he has shot dead the pastor of the local Methodist church. Where do you go from here? In one of his most daringly constructed books, John flashes the story back to the Bataan Death March, which he re-creates thrillingly. I know of no bestselling "thriller writer" today who would undertake such a daunting challenge. John could easily have coasted, but he never has. He takes as much pride in his work today as when he wrote *A Time to Kill*.

There is no popular novelist on John Grisham's exemplary level in terms of range and excellence other than Stephen King.

John's success, his enormous financial wealth, and his fame have never gone to his head. He is one of the most morally centered men I have ever met, and should he go off the rails, there is always his beautiful wife, Renee, to get him back on track. Renee is not only John's favorite companion and mother of his son and daughter, she is also his greatest champion. She is always his first and most trusted reader, tough as nails in the best way possible. When I was his publisher and we would send him a jacket comp, I always asked what Renee thought because if she didn't approve, we were dead in the water. Occasionally, when John fooled around with oddball projects, it was Renee who always told him in no uncertain terms to leave it in the drawer. The great thing about John was that I could be candid and he generally listened. They are an exceptional, golden couple.

Another author that I became very close to was E. Lynn Harris. One day Martha Levin, who ran our Anchor paperback division, marched into my office and, with supreme confidence, announced, "I have found the next Danielle Steele. He is black and gay." "Great," I said. "Can I read something?" "Absolutely not," was the unyielding response.

Martha did me a disservice, but I trusted her, and she turned out to be more prescient than even she realized.

Lynn could not find a publisher for his first novel, *Invisible Life*, so he had it self-published and sold copies out of the trunk of his car. Martha bought his second novel, *Just as I Am*, and it and nine novels that followed all became *New York Times* Best Sellers. When she republished *Invisible Life*, it became a bestseller too.

Most interesting about Lynn was his appeal to a weirdly diverse readership. One could see this when he signed books. The lines were long and they were comprised of gay black and white men, and by white and black elderly ladies. Danielle Steele indeed.

Personally, Lynn was a wonderfully warm, intelligent, and ambitious man. He was scarred by a childhood of sexual abuse. He suffered from depression and heavy alcohol use, and even attempted suicide in 1990. I think writing saved him.

Once he started to earn serious money, family members and friends shamelessly took advantage of his generous nature. His agent, John Hawkins, came to see me regularly to plead for money on Lynn's behalf. John and I ultimately worked out an arrangement where we paid him monthly to regulate his cash flow.

It wasn't easy. We often had so much money out, there seemed little chance of our earning it back. But I insisted we continue to support Lynn, and I think his appreciation was returned by his friendship.

When he died suddenly in 2009 in a hotel room, while on a book tour, it hit me terribly. I don't think I realized until then how fond I had become of this complicated, challenging, and ultimately wonderful man.

10
A YANKEE ABROAD

Cynthia and I were supposed to go to the movies one evening in 1995, but I phoned her to say I had something weighty to discuss, so we had better stay home.

I had had lunch that day with Peter Olson, then not even my boss but clearly angling for Jack Hoeft's job, Bantam Doubleday Dell's CEO.

"How would you like to go to London?" Peter asked as soon as we were seated, clearly relishing my shock

"To do what?" I gulped.

"Become the chairman of Transworld, our publishing house there, and CEO of the newly formed Bantam Doubleday Dell International. All the companies who publish in English would report to you, except America. That means the UK, Canada, Australia, New Zealand, and South Africa. But your prime responsibility would be to acquire a UK publisher."

I admitted to the cheeky executive, clearly having the time of his life, that he had floored me.

"You would have a flat, a car and driver, and six first-class round-trip airfares for two," Peter continued, savoring his come-on act.

Classic Olson. He had thought of everything, especially the glamorous trappings. But what he had failed to do was discuss it with his supervisor and mine, Jack. Not to worry, he said. Why don't you discuss it at home and come back to me.

Cynthia and I had a lengthy, spirited conversation and, typically, she was totally supportive. Her one proviso was that she would spend the summers in the Hamptons, and I would join her there on my vacation. Otherwise, I would go it solo in London in July and August.

The next day I told Peter that, subject to considerably more conversation, I was on board. After we pretty much resolved all the details, he informed me that I would have to go to lunch with Jack and act dumb when he offered me the job. It was without a doubt the greatest performance of my life.

I wasn't at all happy about playing these deceptive games. I liked Jack and felt sorry for him, being duped by Peter, without a doubt the strangest man I ever worked for. Cynthia once declared after spending a weekend with him in Vienna, "that man is an extraterrestrial."

But not in the cuddly ET sense at all. There was nothing endearing about Peter. Rather he was eerie in that he took pleasure in responding to situations and people in perverse ways. Most of us have an innate understanding of what is right and what is wrong, what is appropriate and what is inappropriate. Peter lacked this gene. Sociopath? Maybe.

Peter told us that he grew up in an unhappy home and clearly this oppression colored his ability to observe normal social intercourse. He is cold and remote and has very few friends. He is very smart but only in ways that serve his narcissistic purposes.

When he was divorcing his first wife, he went through an untamed adolescent period, arriving in the office in skin-tight jeans and clinging turtleneck sweaters. In the evenings he trawled Upper West Side bars and eventually settled down with a barmaid of whom he was quite proud.

Some time after that, he met and then married Candice Carpenter, a fellow Harvard grad who became successful as CEO of iVillage.com, which boomed before the bubble broke. Peter behaved like a starry-eyed teenager.

At my 60th-birthday party, friends and I were aghast at seeing the couple smooching in a corner with his hand on her ass. Peter moved into Candice's ugly, cold Park Avenue duplex apartment. They tried to hold salon-like evenings, but they were duds because no one wanted to be there, and both Olsons were rude, inattentive hosts. One Christmas we were all summoned to an open house that was grim. I brought a present and never got an acknowledgment. Other guests told me the same was true for them. Same was true for the chosen who attended their pretentious, over-the-top marriage ceremony in Candice's Southampton estate. Peter had a giant portrait of Candice prominently displayed in his office.

Professionally, it was worse. Peter played by no rules that I could see. He never told me what my clearance was to make acquisitions. When I renewed a Bill O'Reilly contract for $5 million and Peter didn't balk, I blithely decided $5 million was my limit. I continued with this irresponsible behavior until Markus Dohle replaced Peter and gave all of us a $1 million clearance level, much more in keeping with industry norms. Since Peter never appeared to think anything through, his dumb decisions were often detrimental to the company.

His mind-boggling move to take Anchor Books, Doubleday's distinguished paperback arm, and put it alongside Vintage, Knopf's paperback division, to achieve a one-stop shopping powerhouse, was surely the greatest professional betrayal of my career. I was determined to resign, until Robert Levine, my longtime attorney and close friend, told me what it would cost me.

So I hung around, very unhappily. Negotiating the turnover with Sonny Mehta, Knopf's chairman, was a nightmare. Sonny famously disappeared when he didn't want to deal with unpleasant decisions. That, and possibly his being the mastermind of this ridiculous marriage, made him a very annoying absent player. I never knew, nor do I want to know, who was responsible for this appalling decision.

When it came time to renew my contract, Bob and I played payback and negotiated a terrific fuck-you clause that allowed me to leave the company for any reason with three months' notice and a guaranteed golden parachute of two years' salary in one hefty installment.

Peter once asked me if he could excise the offensive clause. I said no. "You still don't trust me?" It's not a question of trust, I told him, more a sense of control. That clause remained in my contract right up until much later, when Markus Dohle stupidly restructured Random House, and Doubleday became a part of Knopf. I have always said that corporations do dumb things. I honestly do not believe that Sonny had any part of this, although he suddenly inherited two of the biggest-selling authors in the world, John Grisham and Dan Brown. Sonny and I were good but distant colleagues until his untimely death in 2019.

Once everything was in place for me to begin a new exciting chapter in my life, I had to resort to some fancy footwork because no one in London knew anything about their new honcho, and the only ones in New York who were in on it were Peter and Jack.

We had to start looking for a flat first. When what sounded like an ideal domicile came up, Cynthia and I embarked on a whirlwind trip to London, took the night flight, went directly to Chesham Place in Belgravia, saw the flat, fell in love with its airy spaciousness, including a reception room with high ceilings and an entire glass wall that opened up to a tiny balcony. It also had a separate dining room, a mammoth master bedroom, two smaller ones, and two bathrooms. The only disappointment was the kitchen, which had the smallest refrigerator I had ever seen. We negotiated and got what they called an American fridge. I called it small, but it was much better.

We went to lunch and returned to the airport for the trip home. Pure adrenaline keeps you afloat on such lunatic excursions, and I was flying higher than the BA aircraft.

Meanwhile, Peter, Jack, and I began a serious search for my successor in the United States. We guessed that David Gernert, the editor in chief, and Bill Barry, the deputy publisher, would have gladly accepted the job of running Doubleday together. They were and are terrific. But they were considerably younger, and despite the fact that they got along well and were liked and admired, we felt they lacked the discipline and gravitas to manage a big publishing house.

We decided to look outside BDD. My first call was to Bill Moyers, the bestselling Doubleday author and public television personality. People forget that despite Bill's time in Washington with Lyndon Johnson, he was the publisher of *Newsday*, the excellent Long Island, New York, newspaper, for three years. I consider Bill a very dear friend, and know he took our unanticipated offer seriously. He even put up with a visit from Jack, one of the all-time great salesmen. But it was not to be. Bill felt uncomfortable about having to spend time on tiresome administrative and managerial duties. I also don't believe he was ready to give up his popular TV gig.

Next up was Richard Holbrooke, then deputy secretary of state under Bill Clinton. Holbrooke came to us via Morton Janklow, the high-powered lawyer/agent. I flew to Washington and went directly to the State Department, where Holbrooke showed off his gorgeous office, replete with a roaring fireplace. After a very interesting tour of State, Holbrooke and I went off to a lively, chatty dinner. Holbrooke could be very charming if he chose to, and he was definitely determined to make an impression on me. He did.

I was able to catch the final shuttle home, and the next morning, bright and early, I reported to my cohorts. "Gentlemen," I said, "bringing in Richard Holbrooke to run Doubleday would be an unmitigated disaster. He wants the job desperately, but it is all about him, not the company, not the staff, not the authors or their books."

I was so passionate, resolute, and credible, Peter and Jack caved immediately.

A couple of days later, Peter rang me to ask if I had heard the rumors that Arlene Friedman, who ran the Literary Guild, a sister Bertelsmann company, was thinking of jumping ship. I had. Knowing her, I offered to call Arlene and snoop around on Peter's behalf. Arlene confirmed she was miserable in the job, and I reported it.

More out of desperation than anything else, we all agreed to trot out the Doubleday job to keep Arlene in the fold. She accepted it on the spot.

I had forgotten that when Linda Grey was looking to replace herself, she considered Arlene as well but finally nixed that idea. "How could I do that to our wonderful staff," she wisely told me. That night when I came home and told Cynthia the deed had been done, her response was prescient: "Wrong!"

Frankly, I always had an inkling that hiring Arlene was a mistake. When I told David Gernert the next morning who his new boss would be, the look of implausible horror on his face, something I will never forget, confirmed my worst suspicions.

Arlene, who died in 2012, was a total pro who had a long and successful career in mass-market publishing, but her sensibility was off-pitch for a house like Doubleday. Her mantra when she took up the reins was totally tone deaf: "mass with class."

Moving countries, I soon discovered, is a bother and a bore. I had to open a UK bank account and do tiresome chores like getting a phone and electricity. The flat was furnished but needed personal stuff, dishes, glasses, flatware. It was endless. Even when I was situated, I always carried a punch list and,

Angela Lansbury enjoying *Mamie's Memoirs* during her run as Mame on Broadway.

On the set of *Star!* Julie Andrews takes a break with extras from the film listening in.

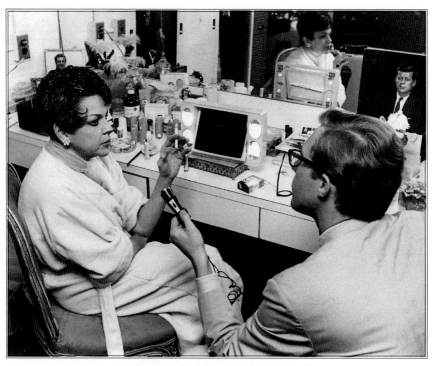

Backstage at the Palace with Judy Garland.

Ginger Rogers, who painted
in her spare time, showing
off her artwork.

Superstar Italian soprano Renata Tebaldi enjoys a stroll on a New York street.

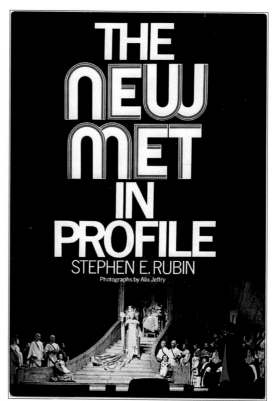

My only book,
published in 1974.

Editorial director
Steve Rubin

Photo by Louie Psihoyos/Psihoyos.com

Jackie O signs up Austin novelist

Book party climaxes dizzying spin to top

By Doug J. Swanson
New York Bureau of The Dallas Morning News

NEW YORK — Less than a year ago, Elizabeth Crook was just another aspiring novelist kicking around Austin. She had a manuscript, no publisher and a collection of rejection letters.

But last week, in a swank Manhattan apartment, here was Ms. Crook, 31, chatting up her editor, Jacqueline Kennedy Onassis. Walter Cronkite stood nearby, talking with journalist Bill Moyers. Singer Judy Collins came, as did actor Tony Randall.

All were there to celebrate the publication of Ms. Crook's novel, *The Raven's Bride*, which is about Sam Houston's first wife. The book party had enough star power to make the

Please see MOYERS' on Page 2C.

Special to The Dallas Morning News: Associated Press

From left, Bill Moyers, author Elizabeth Crook, Steve Rubin of Doubleday and Jacqueline Kennedy Onassis talk up Ms. Crook's novel.

At a launch event for the novelist Elizabeth Crook. From left, host Bill Moyers, Crook, me, and Crook's editor JKO. *Photo by Mario Suriani*

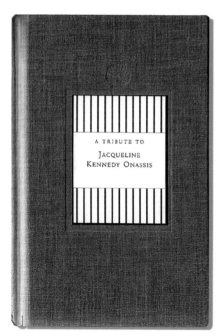
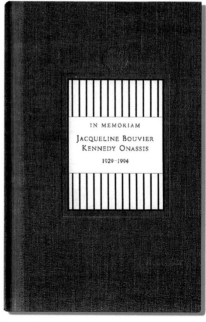

The two books Doubleday published in honor of Jacqueline Kennedy Onassis upon her death.

The publishing division of UJA held a fundraising event
in my honor in 2005:

Three of my very accomplished authors generously gave themselves over to the event.
Pat Conroy, as the master of ceremonies, with John Grisham (far right)
and Dan Brown (far left) as speakers. *Photo by Michael Priest*

A happy honoree. In the background (left) is marketing guru Jackie Everly
and PR honcho Suzanne Herz. *Photo by Michael Priest*

Two colleagues who played huge roles in my career: Jack Romanos (right), who hired me at Bantam, and David Gernert, who was Doubleday's editor in chief, John Grisham's agent, and a cherished pal and drinking buddy. *Photo by Michael Priest*

Me hugging John Grisham after he literally roasted me.
Photo by Michael Priest

My very dear friends Carole and the late Richard Baron.
Photo by Michael Priest

Good things come in threes. At a reception honoring the soprano Anna Moffo, her publicist and soul mate Cynthia Robbins, my wife, is flanked by the author and Cynthia's best friend, Jane Scovell (left), and the great mezzo-soprano Marilyn Horne. Jane wrote two books with Marilyn. *©2006 Beth Bergman*

Three pals are celebrating Joan Sutherland at a cocktail party following a memorial service. From left, Jane Scovell, Marilyn Horne, and me. Horne and Sutherland, two of the greatest voices of the twentieth century, made history singing together. They also adored each other. I adore Jane and Marilyn. *©2006 Beth Bergman*

GEORGE W. BUSH

Sept 28, 05

Dear Steve,

Chris tells me you are leaving Random House. I wish you all the very best in your next venture. I'm sure you will do very well.

I enjoyed meeting you and will work hard to justify your confidence.

Sincerely,

George Bush

I received this gracious and generous note from George W. Bush when I left Doubleday. *Courtesy George W. Bush*

The very complicated change of address notice when Cynthia and I moved to London.

Stephen Rubin & Cynthia Robbins
London
(effective July 7 for Steve, September for Cynthia)

Transworld Publishers	27 Chesham Street
61/63 Uxbridge Road	Flat 9
Ealing, London W5 5SA	London, SW1X 8NQ
ENGLAND	ENGLAND
phone direct (181) 231-6700	phone (171) 235-1879
switchboard (181) 579-2652 x6700	fax (171) 823-1848
fax (181) 231-6702	
assistant (181) 231-6701	

New York City

Bantam Doubleday Dell International	5 East 22nd Street, 26C
1540 Broadway, 22nd floor	New York, NY 10036
New York, NY 10036	phone (212) 353-0866
phone direct (212) 782-9701	(answered 24hrs by a service)
switchboard (212) 354-6500	fax (212) 228-2693
fax (212) 782-8499	
assistant, Vicki Modiano (212) 782-9207	

Long Island
(Cynthia in residence until September)

P.O. Box 461
Hampton Bays, NY 11946
phone (516) 728-0306; (516) 728-8128
fax (516) 728-2276

PERSONS
OF THE YEAR

PUBLISHERS WEEKLY®
PublishersWeekly.com
DECEMBER 24, 2018

For the first time, rather than saluting one person, *PW* is honoring six publishers—all with books related to President Donald Trump, who dominated debate in the country and the industry

Steve Rubin, Henry Holt

Jonathan Karp, Simon & Schuster

Amy Einhorn, Flatiron

Bob Miller, Flatiron

Eric Nelson, Broadside

Rolf Zettersten, Center Street

This 2018 cover of *Publishers Weekly* is filled with friends.
Publishers Weekly *December 24, 2018 cover used by permission.*

For my 75th birthday, I threw a party for eighty-seven of my closest friends at the storied Garrick Club in London. They came from the United States, Italy, France, and, of course, the United Kingdom. Here is a generous sampling from the unforgettable event:

Two of my closest competitors: the late Carolyn Reidy and David Young.
Photo by James O. Jenkins

I attended Alan Alda's spectacular 80th birthday fete, hosted by his lovely wife, Arlene. The Aldas returned the favor and journeyed to London for my 75th. *Photo by James O. Jenkins*

International bigwigs Ricky Cavallero, Georgina Capel, Anne Louise Fisher, Clare Alexander, and Bill Scott-Kerr. *Photo by James O. Jenkins*

The incomparable Sara Bershtel, my esteemed friend from Henry Holt/ Metropolitan. People predicted we wouldn't get on. Were they wrong! *Photo by James O. Jenkins*

Ed Victor attracts the beauties: his wife Carol Ryan, Jane Friedman, Cindy Blake, and her niece, Gillian Blake. *Photo by James O. Jenkins*

Classical music royalty: San Francisco Conservatory President David Stull, retired *New York Times* music, dance, and rock critic John Rockwell, and London supremo Norman Lebrecht. *Photo by James O. Jenkins*

Bill and Jeanne Barry have been close pals since the late 1980s. *Photo by James O. Jenkins*

My friend and author Sebastian Faulks, his wife Veronica, and Patrick Janson-Smith.
Photo by James O. Jenkins

This is how it looked in the very grand and very beautiful Garrick Club dining room before the hoards descended. *Photo by James O. Jenkins*

Nelson and Sandy DeMille flank me and SF Conservatory President David Stull. Sandy died tragically of cancer in 2018. She was universally adored. *Photo by James O. Jenkins*

I am clearly having the time of my life. That's Jane Friedman at left. *Photo by James O. Jenkins*

when I had a free moment, purchased things like corkscrews, salt and pepper cellars, and candlestick holders. I happily splurged on a pricey Bose stereo and TV setup.

Remember, this was the 1990s. I went to work every morning in the back of a midnight-blue Daimler, one of the most beautiful, sleek cars I have ever seen. It came with a chauffeur. When I interviewed a kid named Richard and asked why he wanted to be a driver, he responded, "because me Dad was." I hired him pronto.

To complicate matters further, executives in the United Kingdom have their salaries published by Companies House. Had my salary been made public, I would have been lynched. We are paid considerably more in the United States than they are in the United Kingdom. So we devised a scheme where I was paid modestly in sterling and handsomely in dollars.

Mssrs. Olson and Hoeft handled the Brits with shocking insensitivity, thereby setting me up for an extremely hostile reception in Ealing, which is 40 minutes west of central London. Instead of talking things through with the chairman, Paul Scherer, and the managing director, Mark Barty-King, they just dumped the scenario on them at a sales conference in Florida, and the Brits were livid. Mark and I worked out a decent understanding after I assured him that I did not seek the job but that it had been offered to me.

Not so with Scherer, who I discovered was calling me "Little Stevie Wonder" behind my back and generally poisoning the well. Paul was a legendary and much-loved figure in UK publishing, and we had always gotten along well in the past, but his nose was so out of joint by the idea of an American, let alone a New York smartass, replacing him, and he employed everything in his powerful arsenal to make sure my life would be miserable. He succeeded for a bit; it is very difficult being shut out of a company one was supposed to be managing. People would walk by my office and not acknowledge me. I actually had to insist to Mark that he, at the very least, wave.

Once I figured out what the toxic Scherer was up to, I began fighting back. The Brits can be very difficult to read, especially in a work environment—they are so damned polite, it is impossible to penetrate their real feelings. They are also dead set against any kind of confrontation. But I insisted that my colleagues, most of whom I knew and liked, start welcoming me to meetings and, much more important, spill the beans about what was going on in the company.

Transworld is unquestionably one of the great UK publishing houses, delivering rich financial results year after year. Eventually my comrades came to realize that "Little Stevie Wonder" did not have horns. And when Mark became seriously ill and allowed me to speak to his doctors so that I could report back to his staff, they began the slow process of accepting me. Mark struggled valiantly and gained so much weight because of his medications, his matinee-idol good looks became unrecognizable. At his final Frankfurt Book Fair, he had to stop people and say, "It's me, Mark." He was hospitalized for long periods. At functions like sales conferences, I spoke on his behalf.

His loyal coworkers moved in like the superlative team players they are in Ealing and closed the circle. Occasionally, they let me in, but frankly it was only during Mark's absences that I ever felt useful.

When Transworld published Mikhail Gorbachev's *Memoirs*, Mark was still indisposed, so I took over as the official company host when the Russian leader came to London to promote his book. Gorby, as his wife Raiza called him, came with a full complement of hangers-on, including a very charming translator and an assortment of scary goons, to say nothing of the attractive Mrs. Gorbachev, who was reminiscent of Blanche DuBois in her manner and moods.

We took him to Harrods for a hugely attended book signing, where people thanked him "for saving the world."

Our host was Mohamed Al-Fayed, Harrods's unctuous owner, who fawned on Gorbachev and treated his minders like scum.

In London proper we had the contingent housed at the swank Dorchester Hotel in fashionable Mayfair. One day Gorby cornered me and through his translator asked for a very private meeting for just the three of us. The Dorchester kindly gave us a small conference room. Gorby only referred to me as Mr. Chairman, and I returned the favor and called him Mr. President. So there we were nice and cozy when the president tells me very forcefully through the translator that we weren't paying the translator enough money. It was uncanny. What a piece of political maneuvering. To his credit, the translator never let on in any fashion that he was a party to this act of pure cheekiness. Of course I gave the guy a handsome raise.

But perhaps even more galling was what we discovered when we got the bill for the Gorbachev party from the Dorchester. It seems that every person, except the Gorbachevs, had emptied their entire minibars into their luggage.

Mark and Paul were not at all keen about acquiring a company. If anything, they were hostile to the idea—the order came from on high though and they had no choice but to capitulate. When I told them I was inviting Matthew Evans, the chairman of Faber & Faber, to lunch, they couldn't resist and crashed the party.

We took Evans to a swanky restaurant in Holland Park, and once the quick-witted publisher deduced how uncomfortable the three musketeers were, he sat back and had a fine time. After far too much equivocating, we finally laid our cards on the table faceup and told him we wanted to buy his fabled company. Evans licked his chops and, adopting a faux aggrieved tone, said, "And here I thought you were going to offer me a job."

Next stop was lunch with another Goliath of publishing, Anthony Cheetham. We both walked on eggshells about Transworld possibly acquiring Orion, then his company. Cheetham, a terrific publisher but not always an easy man to do business with, had been fired by Alberto Vitale when he was running Century. He famously went public and announced: "I have been run over by a cockroach." I pointed out to Peter and Jack that the last thing Anthony needed again was another American (via Italy) supervisor.

The only serious acquisition attempt we made was to purchase the scruffy independent upstart Fourth Estate. But the boys in Ealing, chronically averse to change, put the kibosh on it. "They are not like us," they whined. "Right," I responded, "exactly why we want them."

We not only lost a *sui generis* publishing house full of fabulous writers like Carol Shields and Dava Sobel, we missed out on three of the most talented people in the business: Victoria Barnsley, Stephen Page, and Christopher Potter.

If nothing else, I got to know Vicky quite well and even had set up meetings between her and Peter and Jack. They were in favor, but without the support of Transworld, it would have been folly to go forward. Fourth Estate was ultimately bought by News Corp (HarperCollins), and Vicky eventually became their CEO. She was sacked in 2013 for not being able to get on with Brian Murray, their current CEO.

Once Fourth Estate was off the table, my life in Ealing became arid. Yes, I took trips to Sydney, Auckland, Johannesburg, and Toronto, which were informative and fun. But I was bored silly.

The deal I made with Mark Barty-King, to assure his support, was that my involvement in the daily running of Transworld would be "strategic," and I kept my word. I went to all financial meetings and the weekly acquisitions meeting, but that was it. Often, if my twice-weekly mail pouch from the United States failed to turn up, I would become despondent. I prayed for the phone to ring.

My love affair with England began back in 1978 when I was on assignment to do a profile of the director John Schlesinger, who was making the film *Yanks*. But it wasn't until two decades later that I first began to truly understand what it was about the English that attracted me to them and why I began calling myself a "faux Brit."

First, I find England physically very beautiful. I always fondly recall an aimless stroll I took from the embankment entrance of the Savoy Hotel all the way to Belgravia on a beautifully sunny Sunday. All I remember thinking was I want to live here someday. The English countryside is also justly famous for its loveliness. And their architecture is magnificent.

But I am not talking about physical manifestations of the landscape—I have always felt remarkably at home in England, because I think I embraced their people while never trying to alter or mask my very un-British American characteristics. The Brits are not "cold," as detractors will tell you, they are *reserved*. They may take forever to warm to you, but when they do, you have them for life.

Curiously, it was the death of Princess Diana that helped me to understand why I would rather be in London than any other city, except possibly New York.

I was at the gym, two streets away from my flat, on a sunny Sunday morning in August 1997. I was on the treadmill when I noticed all the TV screens flashing incessantly. Finally, I got off to see what the hell was going on.

Incomprehensibly, Princess Diana was dead.

I ran to a phone, woke my wife, told her to turn on the TV, and that I would be home pronto. For the remainder of that momentous day, and for many days following, we sat there in shock glued to the telly. "This is the BBC," an anonymous voice intoned, as though from some celestial domain.

The world mourned "The People's Princess," in the immortal phrase of Alistair Campbell, but to truly comprehend the effect that Diana's death had on her nation, one had to have been there. Time stopped. Floral tributes were everywhere. Traffic around Kensington and Buckingham Palaces was, as the Brits would say, "chokka."

It was impossible to discuss anything else. The BBC coverage was enthralling. Of course, nobody realized it then, but the tragic death of the beautiful, young Diana permanently altered the way the Royal Family operated. Queen Elizabeth, depending on whom you believe, had to be persuaded to address the nation. When she finally did, it was more the speech of a grandmother than a monarch; it was powerful and incredibly moving. Fans of the monarch, none more resolute than me, reveled in her cool but genuine emotion; naysayers were quickly converted.

It is only with hindsight that one realized what a turning point this was for England and the Royal Family. Being there, engulfed in the tremendous outpouring of grief, was a moment in time I will never forget. And it brought home to me very powerfully why I adore the Brits. Beneath their formal exterior, beyond the pomp and circumstance, beyond the royal flourishes, they are deeply emotional and wonderfully genuine.

I made friends in London who remain close to me today. Patrick Janson-Smith, who was in charge of all things editorial at Transworld, may not have been the best manager, but to watch him operate as publisher was thrilling. Patrick, who would come back from lunch soused and sit at his computer with a cigarette dangling from his lips, was possibly more impressive under the influence than not. One thing I learned from Patrick was never to walk away from a project you are committed to.

Cynthia and I would see PJS in the evenings as well. At that time he was living with the Swedish novelist Marika Cobbold, who had purchased Elizabeth David's enchanting town house in Halsey Street, a nice walk from our flat in Chesham Place.

Bill Scott-Kerr, the head of Corgi paperbacks, was a pup then, but his extraordinary talents as a very savvy acquirer and a manager were already apparent. Bill is the man who acquired Dan Brown's first book, but is the least likely superstar. Modest almost to a fault, he just gets the work done and, despite being offered endless opportunities to go elsewhere, is a Transworlder tried and true.

Ursula Mackenzie, who ran Bantam Press and was the only woman senior executive among the boys club, and I shared the joy of jointly publishing Sally Beauman's giant international bestseller *Destiny*. But we became considerably closer when I bought a flat in Kensington, three streets from where she lived. Ursula brought me up to speed on the joys of Kensington, which are considerable, and even shared her tiptop housekeep, Mary, with me.

Ursula and I shared a friendship with Mark Barty-King's widow, Marilyn, and often saw her together. Cynthia and I visited her in her lovely home just off Clapham Common. Marilyn and Cynthia were great friends, and after Cynthia's death, I stayed in touch with her.

Another acquaintance I reconnected with after almost two decades was Cynthia's great friend Cindy Blake. Later we were to have a new connection, Gillian Blake, who is Cindy's niece. The first time we saw each other again was at a dinner party in my flat, and as she came up the stairs, I said, "You haven't changed an iota." Those Blake women not only have great genes, they are great beauties.

While we never got to work with each other, Vicky Barnsley and I have remained good friends. Today, Vicky is the chatelaine of Castle Howard, one of England's greatest tourist attractions. She and her husband, Nick Howard, mostly reside within its spectacular environs. An invitation to Castle Howard is something to be cherished, and the Howards are the most generous hosts.

Cynthia and I were spoiled rotten by the esteemed agent Clare Alexander and her husband Guillermo Gil. We were the strays and Clare and Guill adopted us, inviting us to Christmas, Easter, and all major holiday functions in their lively salon in Islington. I have watched their children, Eliza and Bruno, grow up to be hugely successful, she as a doctor, he as a solicitor. I

have visited them in La Pedrera, a sleepy seaside town in Uruguay, where
Guill has built them a singular and very striking home. They visit me on Long
Island in the summers. They are my closest friends in the United Kingdom.

The only English author I grew close to is Sebastian Faulks. I have been
publishing him since *Devil May Care*, his James Bond novel from 2008.
When I told him at dinner one night, in the presence of his appealing wife,
Veronica, that I was seriously considering buying a flat in London, they went
into overdrive. Sebastian gave me his sister-in-law, Catherine, who is a terrific
estate agent. Far more significantly, Veronica offered to help me furnish the
flat. People often comment on how lovely my place in Sheffield Terrace is
and I always give Veronica the credit. She has an uncanny eye for detail and
exquisite taste.

Sebastian has the dubious honor of being the only writer whose book I
ever edited in its entirety. When I read *A Week in December* in 2009, I got
on the phone with him and told him in no uncertain terms why I was disappointed with the novel. I actually said his hero was boring. After an intense 70
minutes, Sebastian calmly asked if I could put all my thoughts in writing, so
I had to compose my first and I hope last editorial letter. They are very difficult to write. Lucky me, I had the help of Clare Alexander, who felt similarly
about the book.

Because Sebastian's first career was as a journalist, he is never averse to
rewriting. He did a thorough job on *A Week in December*, and it went on to
become one of his biggest sellers since *Birdsong* in the United Kingdom. It
sank without a trace in the United States. I was gone from Doubleday and
they didn't care. I brought Sebastian with me to Henry Holt, where we published three of his novels. Much like William Boyd, Sebastian is one of those
hugely popular British writers who cannot seem to successfully make the trip
across the pond. While we put in an extraordinary effort on behalf of his
novels at Holt, we achieved very modest success.

It fell to me, because of Mark's illness, to begin the search for his successor. My first choice was David Young, then at HarperCollins, but David told me in his most reserved "angel of death" voice that he had been offered the job of managing director at Little, Brown United Kingdom and had accepted it. I was hugely disappointed on a personal and professional level but had to admit that he made the right move. Since then, David rose up the ranks of Hachette, including an eight-year stint as the CEO of Hachette Book Group USA, to become one of the most respected and beloved leaders in publishing.

Much like I felt about being in the United Kingdom, David took to America immediately and flourished there. David may be the quintessential British gent, but he adapted to New York like a native. He is now retired from Hachette but on the boards of Canongate and Scholastic. He has also built himself a home in Umbria, over the hill from where his former colleague and good friend Ursula Mackenzie lives. They take Italian lessons together. The Youngs live in suburban Surrey and David revels in being a man of leisure. I still see him regularly in New York when he attends Scholastic board meetings and, of course, in the United Kingdom.

11
COMING HOME

My guess is I probably stayed at Transworld three or four months too long, but once the powers in New York were begging me to return, I could hardly play hard to get. But I did tell them categorically that I would not return just to run Doubleday. They made me an offer I could not refuse: a new division that would include Doubleday, audio, juvenile publishing, and an evangelical startup.

Cynthia and I returned to the States and to a beautiful Beaux Arts artist's studio on West 67th Street, a far cry from the contemporary, boxy, low-ceilinged Flatiron apartment we left. I like old.

Doubleday was a bit of a mess and was surely suffering from low morale. The new division was all fresh to me, and I had a lot to digest and learn. I was beginning to settle in when Peter Olson rang me one Sunday afternoon in 1998 to tell me that BDD was buying Random House. Since it made perfect sense to combine RH audio and juvenile divisions with their BDD counterparts, my new division suddenly shrank dramatically. But I still had Water-Brook Press in Colorado Springs to deal with, and that proved challenging. It was also great fun to return to the evangelicals, but it was a far cry from the established setup we had at Bantam.

I made it clear to Peter that while I understood their reclaiming audio and juvenile books, I wanted something in return. When it became apparent that Bill Shinker, the brilliant founder and publisher of Broadway Books, and Peter Olson were a doomed mismatch, and Bill left the company, I was given Broadway, and we created yet another division, the Doubleday/Broadway Publishing Group, which included WaterBrook Press. I was finally content being home again.

It wasn't difficult getting Doubleday back on track. They needed leadership and a clear path forward. My first week back, I got a call from the agent David Black, who said he wanted to talk to me about a book I knew nothing about. When he mentioned *Tuesdays with Morrie*, I told David I hadn't read it but that it was a low-level bestseller already. David said yes, but let me tell you why I think Doubleday hasn't begun to tap into the book's potential. He went on to give me a very impressive marketing plan. I took copious notes, thanked him, and immediately called a meeting of the marketing department. We took all of David's ideas and massaged them and actually came up with a more aggressive plan. It was only then that *Tuesdays with Morrie* became a #1 bestseller and the iconic 8-million-plus bestseller it is today. David and the marketing department deserve all the credit.

One of the dodgy inheritances from my predecessor was a very pricey multiple-book contract with Barbara Taylor Bradford, the international bestselling novelist of, among other books, *A Woman of Substance*. Barbara is one of the most generous writers I have ever met. We knew and liked each other but had never worked together. I called her husband, Bob, who ran her career, and asked, "How do we okay Barbara's next book?" Bob said she just writes and delivers it. "Sorry," I responded, "not acceptable. She needs to come into the office and verbally outline the book to me and Carole Baron, her paperback publisher at Dell." Carole has fifty times the experience I had with women's fiction, most notably as Danielle Steele's editor.

The day arrived and Barbara came in wearing the most striking (and probably expensive) blue suit I have ever seen. It doesn't matter how much cosmetic work Barbara may have had done, she is by any reckoning a stunning woman. She gave us a bare-bones outline of her upcoming novel, and Carol and I made some productive suggestions about adding more glamorous locales and warning that her characters can no longer dine on Dover sole and crème brûlée. It actually was a lot of fun.

That afternoon I called Barbara to thank her for the splendid meeting. She asked, "Could you tell how nervous I was?" Why, I asked. "Danielle's editor!" she said. You had to love her.

Barbara's sales track alas was declining. So I called Bob in, showed him the numbers, and told him we couldn't continue at the current advance level. After much posturing and genuine pledges of eternal devotion, he agreed to a million-dollar discount. Later, when it came time to negotiate another deal, Bob refused to come down to a level I could live with, and I suggested they go to St. Martin's, which would eagerly welcome having a name-brand author who was guaranteed to be a bestseller in hardcover and paperback. They were grateful; I was relieved. It was amicable and we remained friends. Bob Bradford had a fearsome reputation. I never had a problem with him. On the contrary, I admired his devotion to Barbara and his strategic plans for her.

Another inheritance I had to deal with was Pat Mulcahy, Doubleday's editor in chief. Pat is a quirky, personable editor, but not a particularly effective editor in chief. Sadly, I had to let her go, and proffered the job to senior editor Bill Thomas, who accepted before I finished making the offer. Bill is a genuinely earnest guy. "I will make you so proud of me," he said. Right he was.

So much of publishing is about great teamwork. But great partnerships are just as important. Linda and I were a dynamic duo at Bantam. Ann Godoff and Scott Moyers are potent partners at Penguin Press; Jamie Raab and Deb Futter are the lively founders of Celadon Books; Gillian Blake and I made music at Henry Holt.

Bill and I were very much in this tradition. Bill is a superb, mostly non-fiction editor with an unerring eye for brilliant narrative books. Together we did a bang-up job on such significant books as *The Lost City of Z* by David Grann. But he was just as brilliant with the novel *The Curious Incident of the Dog in the Night-Time* by Mark Haddon. He also took over an Anchor author named Colson Whitehead and stayed the course with him in triumph after triumph, particularly with his universally acclaimed *Underground Railroad*.

Bill and I are as different as could be. He is considerably more reticent than I am, but I think we respected each other and made our dissimilarities work to our benefit. We are also fond of each other, and that helps. The only time we ever had any issues was when I told him that Spiegel & Grau, an imprint we acquired run by the multifaceted Cindy Spiegel and Julie Grau, had to report to him.

It was a case of disastrous chemistry. Beyond that, Bill seems to have a problem with confident, assertive women. He and Phyllis Grann not only did not get along but often had ugly, contentious arguments in my office. That was okay because Phyllis reported to me. Cindy and Julie reported to him. I insisted that they have a "come to Jesus" lunch and air all their grievances.

When Bill came into my office afterward, his face was beet red and he was clearly distraught. What happened, I asked. "I would fire them for insubordination," was his irate response. "Ain't gonna happen," I told him. From that moment on, those two incredibly talented, challenging editors reported to me. My philosophy in these cases is very simple: if I choose to hire you, I will support you in every case except irresponsible ones. Cindy and Julie are exceptional, and I was bereft when, years after I had left Random House, Gina Centrello shut down the imprint and let them go.

But late in 2020 those indomitable women announced the formation of an independent publishing company, using the same Spiegel & Grau imprimatur. It is exactly what they should be doing: Cindy and Julie are true originals and should not be under corporate restraints, especially a division run by a traditionalist like Gina Centrello.

Once Broadway had been fully integrated into our group, the cookbook editor, Harriet Bell, decided to decamp and take all her starry authors with her. Harriet, though talented, was a negative presence, and I wasn't particularly displeased by her departure, but I had no idea what it would take to keep all the restless authors in the corral.

We had published cookbooks at Doubleday, but it was frankly a very haphazard program. I really didn't know much about what it takes to be a cookbook publisher until I was thrown in the shark-infested waters and learned the hard way to swim. Our biggest star at Doubleday was Lidia Bastianich, very much in the freshman stage of what became a burgeoning career as a relentlessly ambitious cookbook writer.

Bill Shinker was my perfect role model, a fabulous publisher of nonfiction, especially cookbooks. But he was gone and now my authors and their fidgety agents were being wooed by the very editor who had acquired them. We are talking about name brands here: Jean-Georges Vongerichten, Deborah Madison, and Emeril Lagasse.

Thanks to the fact that I had a superlative deputy publisher, Michael Palgon, at Doubleday, I was for weeks on end able to deal with nothing but the mess Harriet caused by jumping ship. We let the authors we didn't care about go with her but kept everyone else. I think it was the only time in my career that I had to battle to retain a posse of authors.

Bill had done a sterling job staffing Broadway with hugely talented editors, marketing, and publicity folk. My real challenge was getting the bottom line into profitability. Like all startups, Broadway fell prey to overpaying for books, and their write-offs were astronomical.

One day the great Jean-Georges came to my office to complain that he wanted more photographs in a book we were soon to publish. I said no way.

Listen, we have actually paid you a fair advance for this book, and if I can keep costs down, we might break even or make a few bucks. When it comes to cookbooks, much like restaurants, every nickel counts. Jean-Georges is a very successful businessman as well as a chef, and he understood where I was coming from and immediately backed off. I loved publishing him because he was not only great to work with, but I think he is one of America's all-time preeminent chefs. His flavors explode in your mouth. As opposed to so many of his fellow chefs who have built thriving empires, Jean-Georges, who was no slouch in opening new restaurants, can often be found in the kitchen of his eponymous restaurant on Central Park West in New York. Lovely guy.

12
THE DA VINCI CODE

Robert Gottlieb, surely the greatest publisher of my time, always jokes that when his time comes, the headline of his obituary will read: "Editor of *Catch-22* Dies." If he is right, I suppose the headline of my obit will read: "Publisher of *The Da Vinci Code* Dies."

Thankfully, books are considerably more famous than their editors or publishers, which is exactly as it should be. Does anyone remember who was responsible for acquiring *The Bridges of Madison County*, or *Watership Down*, or *Lolita*, or *The Grapes of Wrath*, or *The Devil Wears Prada*, or *The Eagle Has Landed*, or *A Brief History of Time*? Does anyone care?

There is no denying that the publication of these and countless other humongous bestsellers were seismic events in very different ways. Surely, *Catch-22* is far more accomplished in a literary sense than *The Da Vinci Code*, which is masterful entertainment. But one thing is sure: both of these books plugged into the cultural consciousness of their times.

I do not consider publishing *The Da Vinci Code* the defining moment of my career in books. I am not sure if I could name a publication that was. But being in charge of such a momentous publication was enormously exciting, pleasurable, and fun. And one which gives me great pride.

Dan Brown's extraordinarily well-crafted novel, published in 2003, has broken all kinds of records:

- It debuted at #1 on the New York Times Best Sellers list, a feat rarely accomplished by an unknown author.

- It sold more copies in its first week than all three of Dan's previous novels (*Digital Fortress*, *Angels and Demons*, and *Deception Point*) combined.

- It has been attacked vociferously by the Catholic Church, which, of course, helped fuel sales. I used to joke that I wanted to write a thank-you note to Cardinal Tarcisio Bertone, who was in charge of doctoral orthodoxy for the Vatican before becoming the archbishop of Genoa, and who called the novel "a sack full of lies" and urged Christians to neither buy nor read it.

- The novel was on the New York Times Best Sellers list for 169 weeks, 59 of them in the #1 slot.

- It has in excess of 12 million copies in print. In paperback it sold more than 10 million copies. Total in print in the United States and Canada exceeds 23 million copies. That figure explodes to 200 million worldwide. These numbers are truly staggering. Very few adult books have come close to *The Da Vinci Code*. *Harry Potter*, for you doubters, is considered a juvenile book.

How did Doubleday transform an unknown, essentially failed novelist into a worldwide superstar?

Let's return to 2001. An editor newly hired by Doubleday, Jason Kaufman, wants to bring one of his authors with him. We read the proposal and it is so persuasive that, despite Dan's foul sales track, we make a two-book offer, not unusual for pop novelists. His previous publisher, Pocket Books, counters with significantly higher dollars, but Dan Brown bravely and wisely decides to go with his editor Jason.

One year later Dan delivers 150 pages of what would become *The Da Vinci Code*, and we send the pages to a broad array of sales and marketing folk for internal reads only. The response is universally euphoric. Most interesting, those early pages of the iconic novel did not even hint at the "bloodline of Christ" controversy that later engulfed the book.

Enthusiastic to put it mildly, we invite Dan to our sales conference and discover instantly what a secret weapon he is going to be. Dan charms one and all with his Ivy League good looks, his undeniable smarts, and his appealing modesty. He is like the professor you wished you had.

The momentum begins to build.

Once the full manuscript is in, we acknowledge that we have something very special on our hands. There is often an overlooked fundamental truth in publishing: *belief.* We never once faltered in our belief that *The Da Vinci Code* was exceptional. Why? Because it was undeniably a page-turner and had a very sexy "bloodline of Christ" subplot and a wonderfully appealing hero in Robert Langdon.

A normal first printing of advance reading copies, even for a brand-name author, is 3,000 copies. We make the unprecedented decision to order 10,000 ARCs for *The Da Vinci Code* for one reason only: we are determined that booksellers and the publishing community read it; that the only way to assure success is to get those reads.

In September 2002 we mail the first wave of ARCs, and we launch our secret weapon, Dan, to meet with top management at the national bookselling chains. Mailings often had different covers. This first one was designed only as a marketing tool, so the jacket contained marketing and sales copy.

The strategy pays off and soon the word is out: *The Da Vinci Code* is the buzz book of the publishing community, and we receive hundreds of phone calls and emails requesting advance copies of the novel. We have succeeded in getting the book read, and the response works in ways beyond our wildest expectations.

As we approach November we discover that our major accounts, responding to the hot and heavy buzz, begin viewing the book in much more ambitious terms. We had announced a 60,000-copy first printing, aggressive for an author whose previous books sold 8,000 copies. But that 60,000 number becomes history when Barnes & Noble increases its initial copy buy from 15,000 to 80,000 copies. Once Borders hears of B&N's move, they up their buy as well.

And here it really gets interesting. Our national accounts realize that, given these huge numbers, they cannot rely exclusively, as they usually do, on the publisher to market the book and pay for cooperative placement. Coop placement is real estate. Publishers pay for their books to be displayed prominently. Instead, the booksellers themselves acknowledge they have to take a proactive role in the selling of *The Da Vinci Code* to their customers. This is, without a doubt, the greatest example of a sales force and its accounts taking ownership of a book that I had ever encountered.

As we entered 2003 we shipped another wave of ARCs, this time with the stunning final jacket, which ultimately defined the genre "Da Vinci books," the many Dan Brown wannabe novels that followed, for years.

Tuesday, March 18, 2003, is the much-anticipated publication date. We have labored long and hard to seed the marketplace, and the results go way beyond our most outlandish fantasies for what we dubbed "Da Vinci Code Day."

Our ground plan for the first week on sale has always been to achieve maximum velocity from day one. To achieve this, we do the following:

- Create a highly unusual ad campaign that employs teaser ads of the *Mona Lisa* with the headline "Why Is This Man Smiling?" Of course, we bought full-page ads as well.
- Acknowledging what a potent force Dan Brown is, we set up a ten-city coast-to-coast tour.

And sometimes you get lucky. Such is the enthusiasm at the *New York Times* that its critic, Janet Maslin, breaks pub date by a day. So we start off the week on Monday with a rhapsodic review prominently plastered in the most important newspaper in America.

"The word is *wow*," Maslin exclaims. "Better than Harry Potter!"

The passionate review sets up an anticipation that drives consumers into bookstores to confront 230,000 books, 1,200 floor displays, *Mona Lisa* posters, shelf talkers, bookmarks, and an unprecedented online promotion on DaVinciCode.com.

It works. On its first day on sale, the book sells 6,000 copies. By week's end, sales ride to 23,000 copies. Most dramatically, the novel lands on the coveted #1 perch of the New York Times Best Sellers list.

We have a bona fide hit on our hands, but that only increases the pressure to manage and maximize our success. We strategize a far-reaching plan to promote the novel continuously through the spring, Mother's Day, Father's Day, summer beach-reading promotions, and the fall. We back this up with a huge advertising and promotion budget.

Every ad we create employs the *Mona Lisa* and uses the "Why Is This Man Smiling?" line as a jumping-off point for:

"Put a Smile on Dad's Face This Father's Day"

"Summer May Be Over, but There Is Still a Reason to Smile"

We soon happily discover that the sales pattern of *The Da Vinci Code* is unlike any other bestseller we knew of. Bestsellers tend to start high and trend downward dramatically, sometimes immediately. *The Da Vinci Code*, on the other hand, starts modestly by bestseller standards and then begins an upward trajectory that peaks strikingly on Father's Day, 13 weeks after publication. Then it begins another upward flight that takes it to its best week ever, a staggering 34 weeks after publication!

Here's how it happened. As a result of the phenomenal sales, word of mouth, and religious controversy the book generated, including some very nasty negative reviews, ABC-TV approached us to help cross-promote a one-hour prime-time special called "Jesus, Mary, and Da Vinci," which used the novel as its inspiration.

At the same time, we announced a contest called "Uncover the Code," in which we revealed that the jacket of the novel has four clues hidden in it. Crack the code, and the grand-prize winner receives a trip for two to Paris.

To set up this contest properly, we suggested to ABC's *Good Morning America* that Dan go on their program the morning of their evening special. They accept. The one-two punch of Dan on *GMA* and the special in the evening catapulted sales to an all-time high, befuddling all publishing pundits and us too, who have never seen anything like it.

To further astound students of publishing lore, eight months after its hardcover publication, we unleashed an illustrated edition of the novel with a $35 price tag, and it took off stratospherically. It was thanks to Phyllis Grann that we up-priced the book from its original $29.95 to $35. She told me I was nuts not to do it, and of course she was right, further proof of my theory that if readers want a book, price is no object. On many bestseller lists we had two slots, one for each book. There are more than a million copies of the illustrated edition in print.

Almost everything about this exhilarating publication broke all the traditional rules. Even all these years after the event, the numbers defy all conventional expectations.

It goes without saying that the Dan Brown mania created by the publication of *Da Vinci* caused all three of his earlier books to become national bestsellers. Amusingly, I got a call from my old pal Jack Romanos inviting me to lunch as a thank-you for the extraordinary bonus he received, courtesy of Dan's two previous books, most notably *Angels and Demons*. That book first introduced Robert Langdon, the stalwart hero portrayed onscreen by Tom Hanks, and was published by Pocket Books, a division of Simon & Schuster, where Jack was CEO.

A book as momentous as *The Da Vinci Code* caused tectonic shifts in all the lives of the principals. Obviously the final rewards were staggering: I got a $1 million bonus one year. If I was paid this, one can imagine what Doubleday, the author, and the agent earned. But beyond the rich financial prizes, there were other benefits. Dan's agent, Heide Lange, pretty much unknown before *Da Vinci*, was transformed into a superstar. Same for Dan's editor, Jason Kaufman.

The book was a runaway bestseller overseas as well. The international publishers who knew one another formed a kind of Da Vinci Club, met once a year, and reveled in one another's successes.

The Da Vinci Code was the gift that kept on giving. Even today. Quite astonishing.

13
RELIGIOUS ENDEAVORS

From day one when I took over Doubleday, I was a great champion of religious publishing. Bertelsmann, our owners, wanted me to discontinue the program, but I strenuously objected. We are making a solid return without a shred of effort, I told them. I want to beef up the marketing and the acquisitions program. I also tried to make them understand that some of Doubleday's backlist religious authors brought great distinction to the list: two pontiffs, John Paul II, Benedict XVI, Archbishop Desmond Tutu, Archbishop Charles Chaput, Mother Teresa, Henri Nouwen, Raymond Brown, Thomas Merton, Joseph Girzone, and George Weigel.

My commitment to religious publishing extended way beyond Catholicism to the evangelical realm, first starting at Bantam, where I learned a lot, especially about how financially remunerative these books are, to Doubleday, WaterBrook Press, and Holt. Curiously, although I published thousands of books on religion, there were very few Jewish ones. I can offer no explanation beyond the fact that none of the editors involved were Jewish.

The very first major acquisition I approved at Doubleday Religion in 1991 was a controversial $2 million for the exclusive mass-market paperback rights to *Catechism of the Catholic Church*. We slapped a garish, embossed, very mass-markety jacket on it and it became our strongest backlist book, an evergreen bestseller, because it sugarcoated a bitter pill of sorts and provided Catholics with an attractive way to be observant.

Once the contract was signed, Bill Barry, who masterminded the deal, told me that Cardinal William Keeler, the Archbishop of Baltimore and president of the United States Conference of Catholic Bishops, from which we bought the *Catechism*, was going to pay a courtesy call to our offices.

"I hope you understand, I am not going to kiss his ring," I said cheekily to Bill.

"Steve," Bill corrected, "you just gave the man $2 million. You have already kissed his ass!"

Bill and his wife, Jeanne, gave me an unforgettable gift to commemorate this occasion, an exquisite pair of socks from Gammarelli of Rome, who have been purveyors of episcopal haberdashery since 1798. They were scarlet red and exactly what an actual cardinal would wear. When I have them on, I feel like a prince, albeit a Jewish one.

Doubleday's religion department embarked on an ambitious and unexpectedly controversial undertaking, to publish the key texts of every major religion, in the most up-to-date translations. When we announced the Koran, you would have thought we were terrorists. Authors threatened to jump ship and wrote the most insulting naïve nonsense. We responded to every one of them and explained the context of a larger program, to publish the most up-to-date versions of the key texts of all the world's major religions. Not one of them left.

Unexpected trouble came from the Church of Latter Day Saints, which refused to grant us permission to publish a new edition of *The Book of Mormon*. It took us two years of intermittent negotiation to finally get them to sign on the dotted line.

Our liaison at the church was a lovely woman, Sheri Dew. She did every-thing in her power to facilitate the union. "They just don't trust you," she told me. About 18 months into this tiresome, protracted mess, I phoned Sheri and asked, "Should I just give up?" "No," she responded, "three elders of the church are coming to New York and would be willing to meet with your folks." I set up a meeting in a large conference room and invited the heads of every department that would be involved. The elder trio looked like char-acters from a 1930s B movie, in their drab, outmoded garb and dour mien. They were unanimous in their refrain, like acid reflux, that we would do their cherished *Book of Mormon* great harm. They never gave us specifics, so it was very challenging to make them feel at ease.

After an hour of this circular rigamarole, I was about to excuse myself when one of the elders asked, "Can we read scripture?" "Of course," I responded. They whipped out copies of their cheaply printed edition of *The Book of Mormon*, complete with a faux leather binding and vulgar gold-embossed lettering. And thus did a bunch of mostly New York Jews read scripture, going around the table twice. Only after this trial did the elders finally agree to a deal. It was a test, and blessedly, we had passed.

But the fun was just beginning. Just as we were about to publish a stun-ning edition of *The Book of Mormon*, Sheri rang up to ask if I would bring the first copy off the press as a gift to the First Presidency of the Church, Gordon Hinckley. I accepted immediately, knowing that the invitation was like being summoned to Rome for a private audience with the Pope. Sheri arranged for a tour of the church's grand headquarters in stunning Salt Lake City, and it reminded me a bit of visiting the Vatican. Finally I was ushered into Presi-dent Hinckley's private chambers to confront a live-wire, 90-plus-year-old Methuselah, with charisma to burn. Jotting down every golden nugget of our conversation were the three elders, dour as ever.

Hinckley and I discovered that we had a love of London in common, and that made the somewhat inane small talk easier. Finally, my host asked if I would sign the gift copy of *The Book of Mormon*.

"First Presidency," I responded, "wouldn't it be highly inappropriate for me to be signing your Bible?"

"Not if you write what I tell you to," the nonagenarian said with a naughty twinkle in his eye.

"I will sign yours if you will sign mine," I said, pulling out a copy of a book of his I had tried in vain to read on the plane.

A definite draw. I will never forget this extraordinary meeting and could easily see why millions of Mormons looked up to this enchanting tribal elder.

The Doubleday edition had a less felicitous outcome. We were charging $30 and belatedly realized, why should they buy our version when they could get the church's edition, hideous though it may be, gratis. I cannot believe we were so shortsighted, but in our desire to include all religions in this far-reaching program, we definitely erred on the side of dumb.

A great honor came our way, or so we thought, when we were offered an opportunity to publish Pope Benedict XVI's hugely anticipated treatise, *Jesus of Nazareth*. We bought the book from the Italian publisher Rizzoli, who had purchased world rights. We produced a gorgeous edition, and all was going hunky-dory until one day deputy publisher Bill Barry walked in to say he had heard from the Vatican. The Holy Father would be grateful if we could do something on behalf of Ignatius Press, his longtime academic publisher in San Francisco, who apparently held an option on all of Benedict's future works. Thankfully, we were able to arrange an accommodation and sold the paperback rights to them at a tidy, six-figure sum.

Three years after *The Da Vinci Code* was published, I traveled to London to partake in one of the most absurd experiences of my life—I was a witness in the copyright infringement trial brought against Dan Brown's publishers by two fellow Random House writers, Michael Baigent and Richard Leigh, authors of *The Holy Blood and the Holy Grail*, which was published in 1982. The claimants said that Dan "hijacked" and "exploited" their book.

We knew that the case had zero merit, and Gail Rebuck, then chair and CEO of Random House UK, tried valiantly to persuade the authors via their agent that this was not only a foolhardy pursuit but a potentially expensive one. In the United Kingdom the losers in such a court battle must pay 85 percent of the winner's legal costs. It wasn't to be. The authors were determined to have their day in court.

And what days they were. Three weeks of them in fact. The setting could have been out of Dickens, taking place in London's High Court, in a tiny, packed courtroom, which threw all the antagonists almost literally into each other's laps.

Justice Peter Smith, bewigged and definitely out of central casting, warned all of us very sternly that no Blackberries were to be turned on. The intimacy of the courtroom did not allow for cheating. Believe me, I tried. Smith had the benefit of being seated above us, like some ridiculous bullying god looking down on his errant flock. Occasionally Smith and I played eye-sees, a very disagreeable experience indeed.

On much-needed and much-appreciated breaks, Dan and the two men suing him often headed for the doorway together. In one bizarre incident, they held the door for Dan and tried to make small talk with him. It was like they were sucking up, trying hard to share in Dan's stardust.

At lunch breaks we thought we had outsmarted the pugnacious British press corps by having discovered a back-street route to our distinguished solicitor's chambers, where we had sandwiches, but like cockroaches, the press with their cameras were everywhere.

One day Dan's bodyguard, a Special Forces, blue-eyed former killer, ordered Dan to get on the floor of their SUV and stay there until he released him across the road from his posh hotel on the Strand, where he was registered under the name of Larry Finlay, his UK publisher.

Dan's then wife, Blythe, was in the States at the express orders of our whippersnapper-smart young barrister, who felt she would be a bad witness. Her absence was cited as suspicious by both the claimants and the judge. Knowing Blythe, I could well understand why the legal experts were wary of her. She did a lot of Dan's research, and they felt, rightly, that under the pressure of an alien court and hostile questioning, she could do real damage.

The rules in British courts are very different than ours. For example, there is a mandate, governed by the honor system, that anyone who is at the courtroom cannot speak to the witness while he is still testifying. Dan was a witness for the defense, and his testimony lasted three days.

It was horrific. In the guise of being perfectly polite, the lawyers for the claimants were asking the rudest questions imaginable about Dan stealing their clients' research in a wholesale fashion. Dan did heroically, but it was long, arduous, and extremely unpleasant.

I saw Dan at the hotel gym one morning and we waved to each other but did not speak. One evening I ran into Dan's UK publicist in the hotel's lobby and thought, *what the hell*: "Tell him he was spectacular today in court," I said to her. Dan later told me that the message gave him great confidence to confront his hostile questioners the next day. He was splendid.

My testimony was very brief. Justice Smith seemed more intent on questioning my genuine ardor for *The Da Vinci Code* than on any legalities. In his opinion the judge wrote that while "my enthusiasm of the book knew no bounds, I am not sure it is as good as he says but then I am no literary person." He sure wasn't, and his attempt to get this case appointed to him drew suspicious comment from the scummy British press. Justice Smith seemed to find the celebrity of Dan and his historic novel of far more interest than the questions of copyright infringement.

Nevertheless, in his designated role, Justice Smith ruled in Dan's favor, saying that the claim for copyright infringement had "failed and is dismissed." The claimants, as expected, were ordered to pay 85 percent of Random House's legal costs, which were estimated at nearly £1.3 million.

Of far more import, the win had huge ramifications for UK publishers. Random House said that the ruling "ensures that novelists remain free to draw on ideas and historical research. . . . Copyright law exists to strike a fair balance between protecting authors' rights on the one hand and allowing creative freedom—literary creative freedom if you like—on the other." It was a momentous ruling for the United Kingdom.

14
MORE CORPORATE CLAPTRAP

One fateful day late in 2008, I was summoned to the office of our new CEO, Markus Dohle. He was very fidgety. Without any small talk, he launched into an explanation of a company-wide restructuring that would affect me because, in essence, I no longer had a job. Doubleday was being merged into Knopf, and the new division would report to Sonny Mehta. He handed me a sheet of paper on which he outlined a new position for me, Publisher at Large, with a very handsome salary, although nowhere near as handsome as the one I was currently being paid.

In situations like this, I tend to be very cool until after the fact. This was an exception: I told Markus what a birdbrained idea this was because the merger would marginalize Doubleday, a great storied company. I have always felt very strongly that corporations do stupid things, and this was a doozy. But there was no convincing him; it was a *fait accompli*. That was that.

"But Stephen, we really want you to continue here, as you can see," Dohle said. I told him what he had outlined wasn't a real job at all, and until he and I could work out something feasible, I was signing nothing. He then trotted out that I would have a fabulous office on the executive floor; I told him I couldn't care less. There was no way I was going to remain on the premises in a fake job.

It took months of intense haggling over lunches and dinners, and we finally arrived at a three-pronged approach:

1. I would continue to work with a select group of my authors: John Grisham, Pat Conroy, Tina Brown, and the novelist Christopher Reich.

2. I would collaborate with Random House UK CEO Gail Rebuck in an attempt to foster greater international cooperation among the disparate divisions in the United States, United Kingdom, and Germany.

3. I would have the option to acquire books and bring them to the three remaining divisions, Knopf/Doubleday, the Random House Publishing Group, and the Crown Publishing Group.

Why wasn't Dan Brown included among my charges? In an act of unmitigated gall and ambition, Suzanne Herz, Doubleday's marketing chief and a close pal of Sonny Mehta's, persuaded me that my involvement in the publication of the next Dan Brown novel (remember, this was post–*Da Vinci Code*), already complicated by Dan's tardy delivery, would only further tangle matters, given that I was no longer on the Doubleday floor and that it was a case of out of sight, out of mind. Herz went on convincingly, asking me why I would want to add a further level of disorder to what was already a Gordian knot of a publication.

She was masterful in her bullying. And I bought it. The only explanation I can offer for my utter naiveté is that this was a period fraught with wild emotional swings, and I surely didn't want to make matters worse.

It was heartbreaking telling Dan we would no longer be working together, particularly after he asked me whether I would still be associated with John Grisham and I had to tell him yes.

Grisham was considerably less diplomatic. "It's the end of Doubleday," he proclaimed publicly. Loyal to a fault, John wasn't entirely wrong. It took Doubleday years to climb out of the shadow of the mighty Knopf. As it was finding its way from being the bastard fledgling to the grander Knopf, I found it very sad to watch such a glorious ship almost sink. Eventually, I found my distance, but perhaps not quite distant enough to applaud their wonderful reemergence under Bill Thomas.

Why Dohle and the powers at Bertelsmann thought that Knopf and Doubleday would make a felicitous match is beyond me. I heard that the long-departed Ed Volini, former business manager to Gina Centrello, and a hugely aspiring if less than hugely cunning conniver, whispered the idea in Dohle's ear. It doesn't really matter. Corporations are always looking to save money by consolidation, particularly support and back-office groups, like sub rights, contracts, legal, and so forth.

Knopf is a legendary powerhouse of mostly literary writers; their list is the envy of any serious publisher. Under Robert Gottlieb, Knopf counterbalanced its more refined authors with commercially serendipitous endeavors like Miss Piggy, Thomas Tryon, Len Deighton, John le Carre, pop psychology, and oversized books about plastic handbags and Hollywood producers. Sonny tried carrying on this high/low tradition, but he lacked Bob's uncanny eye and genuine interest in arcania.

Doubleday has always been the quintessential middlebrow house, reveling in a heady stew of commerce and literature. Herman Wouk, Arthur Hailey, Isaac Asimov, Eugenia Price, Barbara Taylor Bradford, and E. Lynn Harris proudly took their place alongside Ian McEwan, Pat Conroy, Margaret Atwood, Colson Whitehead, Jonathan Lethem, and Bill Moyers.

Doubleday was adept at "making" authors, most notably John Grisham and Dan Brown, but they also established Laura Esquivel, Mark Haddon, David Grann, Tina Brown, and Mitch Albom. I have always said that when

Knopf gets it right, they get it righter than anybody. But Knopf's list is so rich in literary luminaries, they often compete with themselves, to nobody's benefit. That never happened at Doubleday, which had far fewer riches but mined them more rigorously.

When Dohle reconstructed Random House in 2009, he destroyed another fabled publisher and greatly diminished a second: Bantam barely exists anymore, and Doubleday almost disappeared before revitalizing itself. A similar occurrence happened in 1999 when Peter Olson put Dell together with Bantam, thereby eviscerating a great mass-market house. Under longtime Bantamite Irwyn Applebaum, the publisher soon found himself depending on Dell to bring home the bacon with live-wire authors like John Grisham, Lee Child, and Sophie Kinsella and the great editor Susan Kamil.

In an even greater irony, when Olson coupled Bantam and Dell, it was clear to everyone that it was curtains for Dell's Carole Baron. Within no time, Carole moved to Putnam. Much later, she became an editor for Knopf, where she brought them Maeve Binchy and Judy Blume, among others. And soon she was back at her old job, editing Danielle Steele, who often writes three books a year. Carole is paid separately and handsomely for these services, the ultimate fuck-you to a corporation that had treated her appallingly.

I think Random House, no doubt propelled by Bertelsmann, did the most damage of the Big Five by these consolidations, especially in the case of Doubleday, Bantam, and Dell. It remains to be seen whether their attempted purchase of Simon & Schuster passes judicial muster, and if it does, how they will fit the splendid powerhouse S&S into their gigantic, dynamic current operation. Macmillan seems more focused on personnel, ridding themselves of hugely talented older publishers or pushing them into a no-man's-land, being "at large." Of course, there is some truth that consolidation can be a positive move financially, but only if it makes publishing sense. Clearly, I am not objective, but nothing will ever convince me that putting Doubleday together with Knopf makes any publishing sense.

Why didn't it work for me as Random House's Publisher at Large? Why was the nine-month period when I filled that role the only unhappy time in an otherwise felicitous career? It all came down to autonomy.

At Doubleday I had extraordinary freedom to pretty much do exactly as I pleased and buy whatever I wanted. But now, even though I reported to Dohle, I had to go to Sonny, Gina, or Jenny Frost, head of Crown, to get my projects okayed. Worse, with my continuing authors, like John, all plans for him including jackets had to be approved by Sonny. To his credit, Sonny, I think, was slightly embarrassed by this turn of events, and we both tried to make the best of it. Nevertheless, it was demoralizing for me.

The situation with Gina was preordained to be a disaster. To start with, we had a bad history. When Gina was given control of Random House, or "little Random" as the division was known, to the universal shock of the industry, I tried my best to make sure that we would be productive colleagues. At first we seemed to be working so well, I suggested to Gina that Doubleday would partner with Ballantine, from whence she came, for paperback publication on all of our mainstream books, yet retaining our relationship with Anchor on existing and more literary books. For a while, we seemed to be copacetic.

But when I persuaded Peter that Doubleday should partner with Knopf on a limited number of mass-market paperbacks, thereby providing us with an even playing field against Ballantine and Bantam, Gina and Irwyn went ballistic because they were justifiably incensed that the fledgling imprint would hog six of the slots given to mass-market paperbacks. Sorry guys, but this was the only way Doubleday and Knopf could compete in the mass-market realm with the mighty Ballantine and Bantam.

One day Gina rang up to tell me that we should henceforth go our separate ways and no longer do co-pubs together. I felt betrayed, as no doubt
she did by our entry into the mass-market business. From that point on, our
relationship disintegrated, no doubt fueled by my not always friendly characterization of her "betrayal."

When I brought Random my first project as editor-at-large, via editor in
chief Susan Kamil, Gina and I got on the phone, and when she heard what
my involvement would be, she said very forthrightly, "I am too much of a
control freak to let that happen." Adios, Random House.

Probably just as well; we never would have gotten on anyway. In all my
years in corporations, I have done my utmost to play well with others. But I
failed abysmally with Gina. I think it had to do with what I interpreted as her
insecurity. Gina started her career as a managing editor at Pocket Books and
grew to be a splendid reprint publisher under Irwyn Applebaum, who was
then Pocket's chief. The problem is that skill set doesn't involve a lot of inter-
action with authors. If she grew into a more savvy hardcover publisher, it is
because she ceded a lot of hands-on responsibilities to more innately talented
colleagues like Susan Kamil.

Sonny, Jenny, and I all tried to make a go of it. Most significantly, I
did bring them exclusively the memoir of George W. Bush, the forty-third
president of the United States, which went on to sell in excess of 3 million
copies. Getting there, however, was not fun at all and is instructive of how
little Markus Dohle knew in his salad days as the would-be czar of New York
publishers.

The eminent Washington powerbroker and lawyer Robert Barnett offered
me Bush's book exclusively, an astute move by one of Washington's foremost
political strategists. At that point, Bush was hugely unpopular, and it would
have been folly to have him endure rounds of meetings with hostile publishers. By bringing the project to me, Bob, who is a friend, knew not only that

I would behave appropriately but that I could approach three very different publishing houses.

Bob asked me to make Knopf my first stop in the hope of repeating the success he had with Bill Clinton's autobiography. It wasn't to be. Both Sonny and Bob Gottlieb, who edited Clinton, used the same excuse: "My wife would divorce me."

Gina, unsurprisingly, said no as well. So I went to Jenny, who eagerly embraced it. A group of us flew to Dallas, where we had a lively lunch with the ex–frat boy, charming former president, and talked through the book. When it came to making an offer, our strategy was not to negotiate but proffer what we felt the book was worth, respecting our exclusive. That figure was $6.5 million, which Bob ultimately accepted.

Dohle went nuclear. Clearly someone in New York or Germany whispered in his ear about how unpopular Bush was, and that we clearly were overpaying if our first offer was accepted. Jenny and I, individually and together, tried to explain what had happened and why. He wasn't going to be persuaded. Finally, in a moment of pique, I explained, "the horse is out of the barn, Markus. Get the hell off my back."

Ultimately, the book saved Random's year when it was published. It was a runaway bestseller and Bush was a perfect gentleman. I was long gone by then, but there was a great deal of pleasure in seeing my final purchase reap unheard-of rewards. Bush sent me a handwritten note when I left. Classy guy.

The only part of my publisher-at-large responsibilities that gave me any sense of accomplishment was working with the proactive Gail Rebuck, who is not only a savvy strategic thinker but a motivational colleague. We had a ball trying to find a way to bring all the disparate, unfriendly parts of worldwide Random together.

But that was it. Otherwise I was frustrated and bored. Often I shut the door to my posh digs to go shopping on the Internet. Nothing is more depressing than spending one's time trawling the web for bargains when you should be spending big money on books.

Finally, I told Markus I was leaving. Why, I don't know, but he was irrationally concerned about the PR fallout from my exit. I assured him that the last thing I was going to do was trash either him or the corporation, that I had had a great run at Random House for more than a quarter of a century and would say so.

It was true. Despite my utter dissatisfaction with being Publisher at Large, all my varied jobs before then were marvelously exciting, diverse, and extremely fulfilling. Bantam was a romp, a great place to learn the business with hugely experienced and talented colleagues, all of whom were more than willing to share their wisdom. Doubleday was hugely challenging, but thanks to savvy colleagues like Bill Barry and David Gernert, the business was turned around for sure, and I had fabulous authors to publish.

Doubleday is such a great institution in publishing lore. It is thrilling for me to have played a small, but consequential role in its more than 100-year-old history. What I accomplished at Doubleday surely gave me the security to take on my next challenge.

15
FREE AGAIN

I rented an office at Bob Levine's law firm and was so relieved to be out of that cesspool, I was like a kid again. It was exhilarating. The pressure was off and financially I never had to work again thanks to a bountiful, contractual one-time payment Random House paid me. I swore I would never allow myself to enter into a situation that demoralized me again. Frankly, I had no idea what I wanted to do going forward, a lack of pre-contrivance consistent throughout my career.

Thanks to friends interceding on my behalf, I had a great dinner with Brian Murray, CEO of HarperCollins, and an intense lunch with Susan Peterson Kennedy, CEO of Penguin.

Ironically, both offered me exactly the last thing in the world I wanted, an imprint. Imprints are dandy if one is willing to wait for the years it takes to get them functional. Also, imprints are generally established for editors, not publishers. In turning down Murray and Kennedy, I said: "You know what I bring to the table. If you have something broken, let me fix it." Neither had anything they wanted repaired.

The only serious conversations I had were with John Sargent, CEO of Macmillan. We have known each other for years and had regular, occasional lunches. At one of them, which took place during my period of dissatisfaction, I shot off my mouth indiscreetly about how dreadful Random House was, how inexperienced Dohle was, and how the publishing principals,

Sonny, Gina, and Jenny, all pretty much hated one another. Not surprising—you couldn't find three more disparate personalities.

John asked if we should be talking more seriously. I said sure.

John is universally respected for being brave and for straight talking, so it is always a pleasure to engage with him. He once told me, "In my mind, you were running the family business and doing a great job." John's mother, Neltje, was the sister of Nelson Doubleday, and his father, John Sargent Sr., was for years the president of the firm. Once, while chatting, I asked him idly what he wanted Henry Holt to be. "Doubleday!" was the instantaneous response. Right then and there it confirmed in my mind that if I joined Macmillan, it should be as the head of Holt.

It was less easy for John because there was someone else in the job. But after much soul-searching, John opted to offer me the position, and I gladly accepted it.

Then I looked at the numbers, and I almost backed out. I didn't think it was possible to lose $5 million on a measly turnover of $30 million, but that was the gloomy financial picture at Holt. I phoned Bob, my lawyer, and said I would not undertake such a losing proposition. "Don't be a fool," the wise counselor said, "you can only go up." Of course, he was right.

Henry Holt is one of the oldest trade publishers in the United States, founded in 1866. Over its long history, it has published classic books by stalwarts like Robert Frost, Robert Louis Stevenson, Erich Fromm, Philip Caputo, Norman Mailer, Philip Roth, and Erica Jong. In more recent times, it has suffered badly from a messy mix of inappropriate owners and rotten management. In 1985 Holt was bought by the family-owned Holtzbrinck group. From the day they bought it until well into the 2000s, Holt never turned a profit.

Holt is comprised of two imprints, the eponymous division, Henry Holt, and Metropolitan Books. During my time there, the former published a mainstream mix of tony fiction and nonfiction, including Hilary Mantel, Paul Auster, Rick Atkinson, Elizabeth Kolbert, John Banville writing under pseudonym Benjamin Black, Richard Price writing as Harry Brandt, and the multimillion-copy Killing series by Bill O'Reilly. It has also had a run of celebrity books by Billy Crystal, Rob Lowe, and Andy Cohen, who now has his own imprint.

Metropolitan, established in 1995, published an idiosyncratic mix of American and international fiction and nonfiction in diverse subjects ranging from world history to American politics. Its American Empire series brings progressive voices on national politics and policy to mainstream readers. Metropolitan's powerhouse authors include Atul Gawande, Barbara Ehrenreich, Susan Faludi, Orlando Figes, Noam Chomsky, Glenn Greenwald, Thomas Frank, Herta Mueller, and Elizabeth Warren.

I began working at Holt in the iconic but sorely primitive Flatiron building on November 1, 2009. I was appalled to discover a shabby environment with one bathroom per floor. We were on a woman's floor. There was no signage on our doors and a reception area that looked at the back of an assistant's cubicle. It felt like a sordid dump in the garment district. It was also sadly symbolic of the psychological mind-set of a company lacking in confidence and a discernible profile.

But once past the abysmal physical trappings, I was overjoyed to discover a group of deeply committed professionals in dire need of leadership and some rah-rah morale boosting.

I set to work and we got signage, not only for the entry door, but for the big wall in the reception area, which now sported inexpensive but perfectly acceptable Jennifer Convertible black leather furniture. Horrid wire bookshelves were replaced with cheap wooden ones, a few well-placed plants and pictures on the walls and voilà, it was a place you were pleased to work in. The joke around the Flatiron was "Let's get Rubin to do our decorating."

Beyond the externals, there was considerably more to do. Agents were sending Holt their second- and third-level submissions, so my first assignment was to befriend all the agents I didn't know and to remind all the agents I regularly did business with that there was a new player in town called Henry Holt.

The message I gave each and every one of them was: despite Macmillan's well-earned reputation for being stingy, I had John Sargent's word that he would support us in big-ticket auctions. Luckily, a big one came up in the early days, and the agent was Andrew Wylie, which would have major ramifications later. We bid very handsomely for Mark Halperin and John Heilemann, authors of *Game Change*, on their next book. Penguin Press ultimately won the book *Double Down* for considerably more than the $4.1 million we bid. But the word was out that a new aggressive player was around. We dodged a bullet in this case because *Double Down* was a disappointing seller.

One bullet I didn't dodge in those early days was the autobiography of Sean and Leigh Anne Tuohy, the real parents from the book and popular film *The Blind Side*. Holt paid well over $1 million in a heated auction, we crashed the book and shipped 250,000 copies, the largest first printing Holt had had in more than a decade. Much to our distress, 200,000 of those books came back. I like to think that however disappointing, the Tuohy fiasco was a dry run of sorts, to allow Holt to flex some muscles that hadn't been used in many years.

An author whose works have always been published by Holt is the great Hilary Mantel—from her very first novel, *Every Day Is Mother's Day*, in 1985, which was acquired by the veteran editor Marian Wood. When Hilary won the Booker Prize for *Wolf Hall* in 2009, we pounced on this opportunity to give our star literary writer a much more visible profile. When Hilary decided that the two books she had planned on the life of Thomas Cromwell needed to be three, we renegotiated her contract with pleasure. And when *Bring Up the Bodies*, her second volume, arrived, I decided quite controversially to try to package it to appeal to the pop historical novelist Philippa Gregory crowd as well as Hilary's loyal readership. Hilary, always game, went along with us, tarting up her book about Anne Boleyn.

Hilary gave us a surprise Christmas present in 2014 in the guise of a short story collection with the audacious title *The Assassination of Margaret Thatcher*. Rather than offer first serial to the usual suspects, we decided to sell the title story to the *New York Times Book Review*.

They plastered the story prominently, and the *Times* even agreed to publish the story exactly as Hilary wrote it, which meant that the word "fuck" appeared in their august pages, a very rare occurrence.

The much anticipated third volume of the trilogy was finally published in 2020. *The Mirror and the Light*, some 754 pages long, was a huge challenge for us because Hilary's UK publisher, Fourth Estate, treated it with all the secrecy surrounding a Harry Potter book, thereby tying our hands. Nevertheless, the novel appeared in its first week at the #1 perch on the *Times*'s bestseller list.

Our strategy in reinventing Holt was two-pronged: maximize the potential of longtime, beloved authors like Hilary, Paul Auster, and Rick Atkinson while trying to attract some fresh blood.

The most consequential new author we acquired was Bill O'Reilly, the Fox News broadcasting superstar, who had the highest ratings on cable TV and was either embraced as a political guru or hated as a big-mouthed bully. Bill loved to expound on the day's politics, and either you agreed with him or not; when he interviewed people, especially those who disagreed with him, he could be a terrifying adversary.

I had published every one of Bill's books at Broadway, and they were all huge bestsellers. But during my Publisher at Large period, Broadway had let him go to HarperCollins, which released his only modest seller, *Pinheads and Patriots*, in 2010. Over the course of five books, Bill and I had become good professional colleagues. One summer evening in 2010, I had invited Bill to a dinner I was having. At that time we both had homes in Westhampton. Bill accepted, but only for cocktails. When he arrived, Bill asked for a tour of my house, and before he was barely in the door, he started pitching me an idea he had for a series of history books done in a popular fashion "as though John Grisham had written them."

Bill is a very persuasive pitch meister. History is a genre booksellers embrace. When he told me the first book would be called *Killing Lincoln* and described how it would be laid out, I became hugely enthusiastic to say the least. On Monday I called his agent to get a written proposal. When that finally arrived—there was an option to Harper that had to be dealt with—I went straight to John Sargent to say this is a must for Holt.

As was often the case, John thought I had taken leave of my senses. But there was no stopping me. I set up a dinner for the three of us, and only then, after Bill had guaranteed John that no one lost money doing business with him, did John finally succumb.

Neither of us had a clue as to how to value the book financially. I suggested we pay him half of what he was currently receiving for his "cultural" books, $6 million. I guaranteed John that *Killing Lincoln* would sell, I just couldn't say how much. So we bravely took a flyer. Did it pay off!

Through almost two decades working with Bill, I had learned to almost always trust his unerring instincts. Bill is not at all the obnoxious bully he struts out as his TV personality. On the contrary, he is focused, ambitious, competitive, creative, and smart. He can also be a fun date, but only as a twosome—he is surprisingly ill at ease socially. I have always liked him. I still like him.

I loved the idea of a popular history series chronicling the deaths of renowned figures—Lincoln, JFK, Hitler, Patton, Reagan, and, most audaciously, Jesus were to follow. When he proposed Jesus, he was so excited, he had his agent tell me in person, just so that he could see my reaction. Bill didn't realize that I had a long association with the Jesus business.

And just as much as I warmed to the series, I was equally in thrall of the fact that he would use his show, prime time, five nights a week, to shamelessly flog the books and other paraphernalia available on Bill O'Reilly.com. Roger Ailes once said to me, "It's like watching a Turkish bazaar." Roger pretended to be embarrassed by Bill's nonstop salesmanship, but like all of us, I think he was secretly impressed. If anyone ever wrote the book on TV self-promotion, it was Bill O'Reilly.

Such was the success of the series, we actually got to the point where we were paying him an eight-figure advance, with pleasure, because all of us were making unheard of amounts of money. As soon as Bill saw what a cash cow the Killing series was, he became much more involved in every aspect of the books and they just got better and better. He also broadened the concept to include *Killing the Rising Sun, Killing England, Killing the SS*, and the best of them all, *Killing Crazy Horse: The Merciless Indian Wars in America*.

And then the bottom fell out. The first hint of the storm that was brewing occurred in 2004, with opposing lawsuits by Bill against a former producer of his, Andrea Macris, and her lawsuit against Bill, Fox News, and News Corporation, for sexual harassment to the tune of $60 million. They reached an out-of-court settlement in which both parties dropped their suits.

But this was merely an amuse-bouche. In 2016 Roger Ailes was accused by Gretchen Carlson, a Fox Newser, of sexual harassment and was ultimately very publicly fired. Shortly afterward, Fox settled another suit against Bill with a former Fox host, Juliet Huddy, for an alleged $1.6 million. Later that year another former Fox host, Andrea Tantaros, filed a sexual harassment suit against Bill, which was dismissed in court.

Then, in 2017 the *New York Times* took on O'Reilly in a far-reaching, splashy investigative report that claimed Fox had settled five suits against Bill dating back to 2002.

Fox hired the notable firm of Paul Weiss to conduct an investigation. At the same time, almost half of *The O'Reilly Factor*'s advertisers, sixty of them, withdrew their advertisements from the show. On April 19 Fox announced that Bill O'Reilly would no longer be on their network. In October WME, Bill's literary agency, said they would no longer represent him for future deals, and UTA, his TV agents, said they would not renew his contract.

The only one of Bill's business partners to continue with him was Henry Holt.

Our thinking was, first we have a contractual obligation to him. Second, it is not our job to judge our authors. As John Sargent said, "We have published murderers." So we continued on with Bill, to the consternation of many Macmillan colleagues and to the more left-leaning members of the publishing community.

What we soon discovered was that while Bill's firepower was still fearsome, without those nightly plugs, his sales dropped around 50 percent. When you sell what Bill did, even a 50 percent decline is livable. Except that our advances to him, which ranged from mid- to high seven figures and low eight figures, depending on the subject of the books, were all calculated on the fact that he would be pushing the books on TV and were now much too high.

I called Bill and explained that while we were delighted to keep on publishing him, we could not continue at the current advance level. Holt lost a barrel-load of money because of the write-off on his books, and people had to forgo their bonuses.

I had predicted to senior management that Bill is a straight-up guy and would reward us for our loyalty to him by seriously considering my request. He could have hauled us into court and sued us for the money, which would have been foolhardy, but who knew.

In what turned out to be the most stressful negotiation I have ever conducted, with his personal lawyer, who is a very fair and entertaining guy, Bill walked away from millions of dollars and we breathed a huge sigh of relief.

I truly do not care what people think of Bill O'Reilly. I can say with full disclosure that working with him for two decades had been hugely pleasurable, that together Holt and Bill created the greatest nonfiction franchise in recent publishing history, selling 19 million Killing books. Loyalty to Bill goes a long way. So do personal relationships. So does success. Bill is as proud of the Killing books as I am. And I feel a huge debt of gratitude to him for being honorable and principled about bailing out on so much money.

16
PERSONNEL, AGAIN

Beyond acquisitions, I had to deal with some tricky personnel issues at Holt. I inherited an editor in chief, whom I knew from my days at Bantam, but not well. She was a lovely woman who was out of her depth running an editorial department. She was also battling cancer. Nevertheless, I worked out as generous a package as I could and dismissed her. Not a popular move. Then I did something truly stupid and hired a B&N buyer to replace her. She was a disaster and I cut my losses after nine months. Nasty business.

Gillian Blake, an editor who was new to me and who joined Holt about a week before me, threw her hat in the ring. After grilling her mercilessly, I gave her the job in what turned out to be one of the most significant moves I made at Holt or any of my other companies.

Gillian is not only a brilliant editor, she is a delightful person—saucy, funny, and no-nonsense. We evolved into a tremendously effective duo. As Gillian collected more and more successes—a Pulitzer Prize for Elizabeth Kolbert, giant, unexpected bestsellers from Rob Lowe and Andy Cohen, evolving an excellent relationship with Bill O'Reilly and his coauthor, Martin Dugard—she became more confident and began to grow into her role, especially dealing well with the egocentric antics from some of her staff.

I cannot remember an editor in chief who did as many of her own books, while hardly ignoring her administrative duties and mothering her two children. She was impressive in this juggling act, hardly ever losing her considerable cool.

In the marketing department was the formidable Maggie Richards, whom I knew from her days at Broadway Books. Maggie has had a far-reaching career, and all that diverse experience has made her into a powerhouse sales and marketing expert. I used to tease the head of sales that she should pay part of Maggie's salary, such was her commitment to tracking Barnes & Noble and Amazon. It is very rare to find one person who is able to judge submissions from both a publishing and a sales perspective.

Maggie became my invaluable deputy publisher. I have never known anyone who could anticipate my needs as artfully as she did. Since she works 24 hours a day, I used to wake up every morning busting to see my inbox and what she sent me at 4:30 a.m.

We have had some incredible successes and they are in good part thanks to Maggie's savvy marketing prowess. I am talking about the Killing series, Hilary Mantel, Rick Atkinson, Paul Auster, Elizabeth Kolbert, and Rob Lowe among many others.

One of the most satisfying experiences of my early days at Holt was getting to know and learning how to deal with the formidable duo who ran Metropolitan Books. Friends warned me that I would find Sara Bershtel, the head of the imprint, extremely difficult. Nonsense! I warmed to her immediately and I think she returned the favor. It took me much longer to get her cohort Riva Hocherman to trust that I wasn't an adversary. But once we were all enjoying one another, we had a fine time.

Metropolitan publishes a robust group of substantial, significant nonfiction books. When they started 25 years ago, they did much more fiction with authors like Colum McCann, Francine Prose, and Emmanuel Carrière.

As I always teased them, they have yet to meet a manuscript that didn't need either an entire rewrite or extensive editing. They work in teams with often two or even three editors refashioning a manuscript. For a bloated but brilliant biography of Sigmund Freud, Sara spent months cutting 100,000 excessive words from the book.

They are the least lazy, most serious editors I have ever encountered.

Because of their work habits, they published only a small number of books. I felt it was my job to get them to try to reestablish themselves as fiction publishers, and to stop being so timid about spending big bucks for big books. I probably succeeded best in the latter, the breakthrough being Elizabeth Warren's *A Fighting Chance*, for which we paid $2.5 million at auction. While it did very well, it fell short of being profitable.

Nevertheless, Warren was the perfect fit for a program that included Glenn Greenwald, Noam Chomsky, Barbara Ehrenreich, Susan Faludi, and Thomas Frank. Metropolitan has continued their association with Warren, who is a dream to work with.

There was only one case where Sara wanted to spend more money than I did, which makes for an amusing yarn. She gave me a proposal for a fresh look at Laura Ingalls Wilder called *Prairie Fires*. My response was instantaneous and stupid. Nobody cares about her, and *Little House on the Prairie* is way past its sell-by date, I said. She disagreed, and we had a friendly back-and-forth. Finally, I gave in: but not a penny more than $75,000.

She bought the book, it won the Pulitzer Prize in 2018, and went on to sell handsomely, 122,000 hardcover and paperback copies in print. I think it embarrasses Sara, but I tell this story every time I can. It speaks splendidly to how executives often do not know what they are talking about.

The jewel in Metropolitan's crown is Atul Gawande, the full-time surgeon who writes regularly for the *New Yorker* and blesses us with a book when he can find the time. When he delivered *Being Mortal*, we made the decision to try to keep it in hardcover for two years and, with John Sargent's assistance, it became a Macmillan as well as Metropolitan book. The most important aspect of this publication was to get the messaging right: this was not a book about dying, rather it was about the quality of life at the end of life. The book is a masterpiece of its sort, and its success, the combination of our focused marketing and the phenomenal word of mouth, kept the hardcover on the New York Times Best Sellers list for 85 weeks! There are currently 1,237,000 copies of the book in print.

The Metropolitans proved to be genuine heroes when they jumped into the fray and helped salvage Holt's publication of the great leaker, Edward Snowden's *Permanent Record*.

The first call came to Gillian Blake. It was from a high-ranking ACLU lawyer, who told her he was representing Edward Snowden, and because of the extreme sensitivity of the subject matter, was only getting in touch with people he knew and trusted. He and Gillian had been at Harvard together. As the project's literary agent, he chose Chris Parris-Lamb of the Gernert Company, again because he knew him. He was only submitting to one other editor, at Random House, yet again someone he knew.

We immediately signaled our enthusiastic interest and soon traveled to Chris's office to Skype with Ed. There were all kinds of technical glitches, but once we got through to Ed in his room in Moscow, it went very well.

Ed is a charmer, very smart, and of course totally paranoid about any-thing involving the web. And why not? Who knows more about leaks than the great leaker Edward Snowden? For a while, Ed was public enemy number one to a large percentage of Americans, who never forgave him for leaking such sensitive documents.

He was very convincing as a potential author, as were we with John and Don, and we went into an auction of sorts with Random House and paid a hefty mid-seven-figures sum to become the winners.

Then the complications really began. The ACLU lawyer insisted that the deal be done through a German company, which was challenging, but we did it. Correctly fearing the US government's intrusion, they insisted on receiving all monies due them upon acceptance of the manuscript. We managed that too.

Ed insisted we only communicate through encrypted files, and that nothing he sent us could ever be copied on a printer attached to the web, which meant all modern printers. We actually had to locate and purchase an old-fashioned printer that regurgitated pages one at a time and had no connection to anything except olden days.

All of this cloak-and-dagger stuff also involved many plane trips to Moscow by Ed's lawyer.

The manuscript was surprisingly accomplished. Ed had written it, and they hired a talented young novelist to help give it some spunk and shape.

By the time we were ready to edit it, Gillian was long gone and we asked the Metropolitans to take over the project. They did without hesitation, except, of course, for the hefty advance, and they announced that three editors, Sara, Riva, and Grigory Tovbis would jointly work on the book, the latter specifically on translating complicated technical material into accessible layman's terms. They all worked nonstop for weeks and took a solid B manuscript and transformed it into an A-plus engaging page-turner.

In all, the publication was a success and all of us involved were very proud of having brought the book to the reading public. But I misjudged the interest in Ed's story. When we announced it, I expected front-page headlines. Wrong. We got plenty of coverage but nothing like I anticipated. Just short squibs. The book was on the New York Times Best Sellers list for 5 weeks and has 197,000 hardcovers and paperbacks in print, nothing to be ashamed of. But it's nowhere near enough copies for us to break even let alone make a profit. I was convinced we could sell well north of 500,000 copies.

Understanding the math here does not take a degree from Wharton. We pay an author an advance against royalties. Royalties for hardcovers are generally 15 percent of the cover price. Publish a book for $30 and the royalty is $4.50 per book. Now just do the math. I was seriously off-base.

17
FIRE AND FURY

It all started at a meal. Blessedly, this was dinner, which meant that we not only had fine food but fine wines, scotches, and bourbons. It was November 2016, and there were three of us, an editor, a writer, and me, all foodies and boozers, and we were celebrating a just-concluded deal, a book about Roger Ailes. Over cocktails, wasting no time, the writer astonished us with the news that he'd become friendly with Steve Bannon, and that in the wake of Donald Trump's election, Bannon might be able to get him access to the White House. That writer, of course, was Michael Wolff, and his momentous book was *Fire and Fury*, of which one wag said, "*Fire and Fury* is the book that ate Washington."

In early January Michael told us that he would indeed be given access to the White House; soon after that, Michael delivered a smashing proposal, and we immediately signed up the book.

Michael's goal—he is famously fast—was to deliver a rough draft of the book by early September, and he pretty much met it. The narrative had a number of holes, and the last couple of chapters were incomplete. But Michael and his editor, John Sterling, did an enormous amount of work through that fall, and by mid-November it went off to the printer.

By mid-October we knew we had a terrific book on our hands. I even thought we had a shot at selling a million copies. We pitched the book to the key salespeople in December. They were wide-eyed with excitement—wow, the first book that takes us inside the insane Trump White House! Suddenly everyone was on board, and by Christmas the entire company was behind the book.

Pub week—or, more accurately, the week leading up to our official pub date—was probably the wildest experience of my career. Everything broke perfectly, Trump threatened to sue, and the rest is history.

We always planned for *Fire and Fury* to be a #1 bestseller. We ordered a 150,000-copy first printing, a huge number in a challenging marketplace, especially with an author who was not well known. In our minds there was only one question: How big a bestseller would the book be?

Given its startling and breaking news content, we had to embargo *Fire and Fury*. But that embargo was broken by the *Guardian*, the diligent UK newspaper, and the very next day President Trump's lawyer sent me and Michael a baseless, insulting, bullying cease-and-desist letter.

This was a gut check.

For all of us at Holt, the commitment to *Fire and Fury* by our owner, Holtzbrinck, and our parent company, Macmillan, had been absolute. CEO Stefan von Holtzbrinck, Macmillan CEO John Sargent, and President Don Weisberg read the manuscript and were resolutely committed to the book.

They vowed to proceed with the book, despite Trump's idiotic threat, and we moved the publication date to the very next day, thereby making an unequivocal commitment to the First Amendment rights of Michael Wolff, Macmillan, and all authors across the land. We also sent a very stern response to the president's lawyers, telling them in no uncertain terms to fuck off. That ended our correspondence, because like all bullies, they backed off at the first sign of a real fight.

Once the book was out there, Michael did yeoman's work in standing up to a lot of intense pressure and some tough personal criticism, while taking on the planet's foremost bully.

Here are some delectable factoids about *Fire and Fury*:

- There are 1.5 million copies of the hardcover in print, accumulated over 23 printings.
- 750,000 e-books have been sold.
- There are 315,000 copies of the audiobook in print.
- The hardcover was on the New York Times Best Sellers list for 16 weeks, debuting at #1 and lodged at the top perch for 9 weeks.
- Rights to the book have been sold to thirty-five countries including France, Germany, Israel, Russia, Turkey, and Vietnam. In the United Kingdom and Ireland, it was a #1 bestseller.

These figures are very impressive and remind me why so many veterans remain in the book business. In an era when social media and cable television dominate the conversation, it is thrilling that one lone book could cut through all the static and have a profound effect on an entire nation. It is surely the first work to spark an urgent debate about Trump's fitness for office.

Because Michael has been writing books and articles for decades without worrying about offending people, he is the first to acknowledge that he has lots of enemies out there, including many journalists. To put it as directly as I can, I strongly believe that his peers were jealous because no one but Michael would have had the gall to even suggest what he did to the Trump folks, let alone to have it accepted and then to transform total anarchy into a classic, historic work of investigative journalism, written with verve, wit, and panache.

In an astonishing article for the *New York Times*, the opinion columnist Ross Douthat compared the much-anticipated Mueller Report to *Fire and Fury*: "one way to approach the Mueller Report . . . is to see it as a more rigorous, capacious version of *Fire and Fury*."

Starting in early January 2018 and continuing for about a month, Michael tirelessly made the rounds to the expected suspects: the *Today* show, *Meet the Press*, *CBS This Morning*, Stephen Colbert, *Morning Joe*, Lawrence O'Donnell, *The View*, Smerconish, NPR, Bill Maher, and *The Daily Show*. Whether friendly or hostile, Michael just forged ahead.

The reviews were all over the place, and what I found annoying about a great number of them was that even though they couldn't resist calling Michael to task for sloppy reporting or some such thing, they also could not hide their begrudging admiration for the book as a great romp. Here is NPR:

"In response to Trump's claim that *Fire and Fury* is a 'phony' book, Wolff said, 'my credibility is being questioned by a man who has less credibility than perhaps anyone who has ever walked on Earth at this point.' It's a classic Trumpian move—not addressing the actual criticism, while maintaining that your enemy is way worse. 'Media is personal. It is a series of blood scores,' Wolff notes at one point. Apparently.

"So read it, sure—but as the commercials say, only 'as part of a balanced diet.' Much of the narrative is not substantively different from information found in other reporting on the president. But many other reporters have been restrained and careful where Wolff is shameless. Facts, Wolff appears to think, have done nothing to hurt Trump—so he is fighting spectacle with spectacle."

Or *Entertainment Weekly*:

"But Wolff's lasting achievement here is not his headline-grabbing revelations but the skillful, enthralling, and utterly terrifying way he depicts the unqualified, unprepared, and downright unusual characters to be found wandering the halls of the White House in the first half of 2017 as well as their near bloodsport-level conflicts. Spicer was right. You really can't make this sh– up, though, long before the end, many readers will wish *Fire and Fury* could be filed under 'Fiction.' B+"

Finally, Masha Gessen in the *New Yorker*:

"Wolff's book seems to occupy a middle ground: between the writing of White House newspaper reporters, who exercise preternatural restraint when writing about the Administration, and the late-night comedians, who offer a sense of release from that restraint because they are not held to journalistic standards of veracity. That middle ground, where there is neither restraint nor accuracy, shouldn't exist. That 'Fire and Fury' can occupy so much of the public-conversation space degrades our sense of reality further, while creating the illusion of affirming it."

When interviewers gleefully trotted out the nasty reviews, Michael dealt with them with dispatch. He shlepped to Philadelphia and Washington. He was peripatetic, marvelous, and, I thought, very effective. And tireless.

Of course, we laid out a fortune in COOP placement, so the book was front and center everywhere. For more than a month, it was humanly impossible to miss *Fire and Fury*. It was a triumph for Michael and for Holt. It was also exhilarating and fun.

Having been the publisher of *Fire and Fury* meant that I saw every anti-Trump proposal on the block, often on an exclusive basis. I have lost count, but I think I got at least five phone calls from different representatives about a Michael Cohen book. I said "no, thanks" to all of them. Way too unreliable a source for me.

Beyond a doubt, the best call of all was an offer to have the first meeting with Michael Avenatti, who was representing Stephanie Clifford, otherwise known as Stormy Daniels. No way was I going to miss out on this one, and we sandwiched a quick meeting in at lunchtime.

Avenatti was captivating. Slick, cool, confident, and spectacularly sleazy, he was hugely pleased with himself, especially when he strutted, "Wanna know why I took her on as a client?"

"Sure."

"She asked me why I would represent a woman who sucks cock for a living. I thought that took balls and I respected her for it."

The meeting was interrupted by Avenatti taking innumerable phone calls, even walking into the hall for privacy. I guess he was there no more than 15 minutes.

Later, I called his agent, Luke Janklow, and told him that while I was interested, my staff threatened to resign en masse if I pursued it.

I encountered the same overwrought response when we met with former press secretary Sarah Huckabee Sanders. I was wily enough to set the meeting on another floor, but Sanders arrived early and we had no choice but to see her in full sight of the Holt staff.

I thought she was great. First off, she is much more together-looking than she appeared on television. She is also charming, smart, and very funny.

Here's why I thought her book would have a huge audience among conservative women: Sanders stood by her man.

That evening at the elevator bank, when leaving the office, I was glared at by a woman I didn't know who finally accosted me and said: "You are not going to publish that woman, are you?" I just shrugged as we entered the elevator.

Ultimately we lost the book to sister company St. Martin's, because Sanders's dad, Governor Mike Huckabee, recommended them, having had a happy publishing experience with them himself.

Simon & Schuster's CEO Jonathan Karp almost had an insurrection on his hands when the company acquired the autobiography of Mike Pence. Karp masterfully fielded hostile questions in a town hall Zoom format that seemed to calm the insurrectionists.

I remember when employees at Macmillan refused to work on books by Bill O'Reilly, and CEO John Sargent in the nicest way possible suggested they find work elsewhere. No one quit.

One of the very few things I missed from my days at Doubleday was the religious publishing program. I decided I would dip a toe into the holy water by acquiring a full-fledged biography of Pope Francis by the eminent British journalist Austen Ivereigh. We called it *The Great Reformer* and plastered a wonderfully sunny photo of the Holy Father on the jacket. Austen is fluent in Spanish, which allowed him to interview Francis in his native language. The result was an unusually human, accessible, and mildly controversial book, and it performed handsomely.

When Austen came to town to promote it, he was invited to breakfast by Archbishop Timothy Dolan of New York. He brought along his agent, Bill Barry, his marketer Maggie Richards, and the token Jew, his publisher—me. I had been trying for years to convince Dolan to write a book because he is so flamboyantly hammy. He makes Bing Crosby in *Going My Way* look like a retiring wallflower.

Before we ate, the holy quartet attended early morning mass in the imposing and overwhelmingly beautiful St. Patrick's Cathedral. I followed the lead of my Catholic cohorts, except for crossing myself, and found the ceremony powerful. There are theatrical elements to a mass that appeal very much to my own theatrical instincts.

The cardinal's quarters are just behind the mighty house of worship, and we were greeted warmly by the gigantic proportioned Dolan, who proudly showed off his glam digs, especially a table he has displaying red cardinal hats, including one from the St. Louis ball club.

When we were invited to sit down for breakfast, two marvelous, elderly Irish ladies fussed over us with enough food to feed a small army. They brought out a huge platter of smoked salmon, and the cardinal beamed. "Please help yourselves to some Jewish bacon," he intoned. Dolan clearly has a rich repertory of wisecracks, and they are delivered with such charm and energy, you would have to be a sour skeptic not to be taken in by it all. For the former yeshiva boy who had just been to his first mass, I was gobbling up every morsel. I admit that for a completely secular person, I seem to be mightily attracted to things Catholic, especially the masses and requiems of Mozart and Verdi.

I never succeeded in wrenching a book out of Dolan, but my splendid relationship with Austen resulted in a second book about Francis, *Wounded Shepherd*, and, much more momentously, an extraordinary book by the Pope himself.

18

BAD MANAGEMENT

In 2018 Macmillan's senior management embarked on a far-reaching attempt to solve all of its succession strategy issues with its older leaders. The key principals involved were Sally Richardson, Jonathan Galassi, and me. Don Weisberg, the president of Macmillan, was very clear that he wanted me to stay as long as I wanted, but that if I chose to leave, he needed to have a plan in place. As a great champion of succession strategy, I embraced the assignment.

In discussing who might be appropriate for the job, I told him in no uncertain terms that my first choice would be David Drake at Crown, but that I worried he would not leave until Barack Obama's presidential memoir was published. We jointly decided that while he was an excellent candidate, we didn't want to get into a long imbroglio with Drake.

He asked me about our editor in chief Gillian Blake, and I told him that while I adored Gillian, she never sent me any signal that this was her desire. Big mistake.

We then discussed other candidates, and he asked me if I would meet with a juvenile publisher he worked with for years at Penguin, who was busting to run an adult division and had written two adult novels, one of which was published by Farrar, Straus & Giroux. He also said that this person was very savvy about creating original content. He sounds interesting, I said, sure.

It is very important to understand that this was the extent of what Don told me. Since my hiring of Ben Schrank was the worst personnel disaster of my career—I think even worse than Bertelsmann hiring Paul Neuthaler—and everyone thought Weisberg rammed Schrank down my throat, I want to be very clear: the decision was mine and mine alone.

I began to interview a varied group of candidates, including Schrank. Of them, he was the most passionate to have the job, something that in the past has always influenced my decisions. I had many disappointments when people I spoke to wanted to remain in their current positions. The more we spoke, the more I liked Schrank, and what finally persuaded me to support him was a long, somewhat boozy dinner where we played off each other dramatically. It was immediately apparent that we were opposites: he was introverted, withdrawn, and barely spoke above a whisper; I am brash, opinionated, and a bit of a loudmouth. The next day Schrank told me he couldn't sleep a wink, he was so excited. That did it. We set up a meeting for John Sargent to interview him. John, as always, was supportive but was clear about the negatives: Schrank's inexperience and his shy, quiet personality. Nevertheless, I hired him.

From then on, it was dominoes falling.

First, I don't think I appreciated the finality of my ceding my job to someone else. By any reckoning, hiring Schrank happened very quickly. No doubt too quickly. I never really thought of myself as retiring, just lessening my workload. But I am not sure if I was clear of that in my own head, or what I communicated to Don or others.

When I told my senior staff who their next boss would be, the reaction was unlike anything I have ever seen. Gillian Blake simply went bonkers; Sara Bershtel was stupefied; Maggie Richards tried very hard to be supportive. When the news became public, all of Gillian's supporters, who are legion, turned the decision into a political hot potato—I had hired a white guy with no experience over a talented woman.

Then, I was told that a former employee of Schrank's who worked at Macmillan called around to some assistants at Holt and warned them to *run* because Schrank was difficult and a total control freak.

I made it my business to warn Schrank with total candor that he was about to walk into a calamitous situation, and that he needed to confront it all head-on. Schrank, curiously, seemed unperturbed.

This cool attitude perplexed me. Was the guy an ostrich or cocksure?

In my mind Schrank's priority was to try to establish a rapport with Gillian. Instead, he ignored her. When she told me after a week that he hadn't contacted her, I queried him and he said he would. That relationship was never to be.

Schrank spent a lot of time on contacting agents and setting up meetings. When someone told me that he brought his assistant to these meetings, I asked him about it, and he admitted he had but would cease doing it. It is utterly ridiculous meeting new agents with your assistant in tow.

When he went on a predetermined holiday, he told me but not his staff, I knew for sure that something was seriously wrong with this guy.

Lots more to come. One night I was passing his office and saw that he left a very confidential manuscript on his desk overnight. To show where my head was by this point, I could have removed the sensitive document but didn't in the hope that someone would find it and I would have grounds to sack him.

I called a meeting of John and Don and told them we need to cut our losses and get rid of this guy. They were very clear that we needed to give him more time to learn the ropes. I told them he would do nothing but further damage, that his staff was demoralized, and while nobody disliked him personally, he could not do the job.

Then John, without consulting me, put him in charge of the challenging publication of *Permanent Record* by Edward Snowden, and that really showed his true colors. He actually was stupid enough to tell someone he intended to cut me and Maggie out of the process. I was easy, because I rarely descended into the weeds, and he essentially succeeded, but Maggie was in charge of marketing and PR, so little hope there.

As Schrank continued to baffle everyone, Gillian left Holt to go to Crown, working for David Drake. I finally spent a weekend writing the Case Against Ben Schrank and presented it verbally to John and Don.

A publisher, first off, needs to be a leader. He needs to have a clear strategy for what kind of list he wants to produce. Then he needs to be able to verbalize this to his staff and always be available to them. And he needs to be a rainmaker and attract great projects to the house. Schrank failed dismally in every one of these prerequisites.

John and Don told me I was very convincing, and on a bright Thursday morning at 9:30, Don sacked Ben Schrank, who was never again seen at Holt.

The relief was very temporary, because Don was determined to replace him quickly. He asked me what I thought about Amy Einhorn, who was the publisher at Flatiron Books. I asked if he was willing to pillage one company to salvage another. He said yes. I offered to speak to Amy, and we had a brief 20-minute chat, where I told her coming to Holt would be a win-win:

Holt was weak in fiction, she was strong; her career track would never have included a house like Holt. It all happened over a weekend. Included in that weekend was the first and only contentious conversation I ever had with Don. He asked me how I would feel reporting to Amy in my special capacity to acquire some big books for the company. I told him he must be out of his mind, why would I end an admired career reporting to a subordinate colleague. That could have been it for me and Weisberg, the end of a cherished 30-year friendship, but Don wrote to me well after the ugliness and we had a couple of agreeable e-chats and even a dinner.

It has taken me months to come to grips with the Schrank fiasco. Here is how I see it: I made a dreadful mistake. But I cannot believe that Don would have so warmly recommended someone with such obvious flaws. It truly baf-fles me. I used to blame myself 100 percent. Now I give Don 25 percent. When I mentioned this to John, he said he thought Don blamed himself considerably more.

With hindsight, I believe that the nine months Schrank was at Holt did the company immeasurable damage. First, we lost a superb editor in chief in Gillian. Second, the staff was demoralized. If they had disliked Schrank, it would have been easier, but he is a likable guy. His trotting all over town lost Holt credibility with the agent community. When he tried finding a replace-ment for Gillian, every single person was only interested in his job, as nobody wanted to report to him.

Of course people were polite with me, but they must have thought I had taken leave of my senses. I don't care about my reputation—it will survive even a blunder of this proportion. But I do seriously care about Holt, and they suffered mightily under his non-management. Under Amy, it is just a different company, much more like its sister companies at Macmillan. And Amy had the same problem Schrank had in finding a new editor in chief. In a move of unconscionable cruelty, Amy publicly demoted Serena Jones, the current incumbent, to executive editor. This move caused publishing folk who didn't even know Serena to take her side.

In all my happy years at Macmillan, I never thought of it as an inhumane place. Amy was unthinkably impetuous.

Amy and I behaved impeccably with each other. However, in all the time I was around, she never asked me a single question about personnel, authors, or any other germane issue. All she told me was that she was a control freak and didn't want to continue with Bill O'Reilly. I figured that out for myself.

Don and I began trying to find another way for me to stay at Macmillan. I believe he was genuine, and I tried too. But it was doomed. In the midst of negotiating a potential position, I called my lawyer and said I want out, and she said, "I don't blame you. They are behaving rottenly toward you." On my very last day at the company, I had lunch with a competitor who dangled a job offer. After that lunch Macmillan's hugely incompetent human resources director treated me as if I were a thug and was attempting to rob the company of confidential material. It was ghastly, a grim way to close what had been a wonderful relationship.

When it came to hiring an editor in chief, it was a shock to me that Amy named Sarah Crichton as her appointment. Sarah had recently been sacked by sister company Farrar, Straus & Giroux. Did Amy check with them first? Not to my knowledge. Only time will tell which company was correct in their assessment.

Amy herself is a successful publisher of commercial fiction. But does she have the breadth of interest and understanding to run Holt's wide-ranging list? I think not. My view is that she should have her own imprint to publish the sort of books at which she excels. She is way too lightweight for Holt.

In his entire time at Holt, Schrank only acquired one book, an oral history of HBO. He was also responsible for hiring an excellent new art director.

In September of 2020 the publishing world had to grapple with the incomprehensible news that one of the most respected and admired CEOs in the business was leaving his post after a titanic disagreement with the owner of the company.

John Sargent was the heart and soul of Macmillan, an executive universally adored by his confreres, an executive totally committed to his boss, the owner, Stefan von Holtzbrinck, CEO of the Holtzbrinck Publishing Group. It was Stefan who announced John's mind-boggling departure.

I saw firsthand John's uncommon loyalty to his boss: his getting on a plane at Stefan's last-minute request; his interrupting a jam-packed schedule to take interminable phone calls from Germany. John and Stefan were not only like pages in a book, they seemed genuinely fond of each other.

The principals are safeguarding whatever their disagreement was, but one thing we know: whatever it was is off the table. So after making the dumbest move in recent publishing history, Stefan is not going to get his way anyway.

John is one the most decent, upstanding, fearless leaders I have ever worked for. And he never lied. Of how many CEOs can you say that? He was also that rare higher-up who understood that a smart publishing decision is not always synonymous with a smart business decision. His departure was a dark day for Macmillan.

It came as no surprise that Don Weisberg was chosen to replace him. Don is an experienced veteran when it comes to sales, marketing, and operations. He was also responsible for motivating Macmillan's publishers to be considerably more aggressive and competitive.

My Last Act

Much to my surprise and delight, when it was announced that I was leaving Macmillan, two competing companies came knocking on my door. I was particularly grateful that Jonathan Karp, then the president and publisher of Simon & Schuster, was interested in finding me a position working for him. For years, Jon and I have run a mutual admiration society.

We often competed against each other in auctions and seemed to have a similar philosophy about publishing. We had occasional lunches, which were always great fun. For a guy who doesn't drink, Jon was also a vibrant star at dinner parties.

We finally landed on a very loosely defined "consulting publisher" position and managed to work it out ourselves rather than involving his boss, my dear friend, Carolyn Reidy, which would have been uncomfortable and inappropriate. My mandate was to bring in high-visibility projects and to be available as a consigliere. Seemingly within no time, Carolyn tragically died and Jon was promoted to replace her.

On the momentous morning of May 12, 2020, my phone rang at around 9:30 in the morning and it was Dennis Eulau, Simon & Schuster's COO, whom I had never spoken to. As gently as he could, he informed me that Carolyn had had a heart attack and had died, and that they were very concerned about her husband, Stephen. They knew that I was close to the Reidys and lived 20 minutes from them in the Hamptons. We were all quarantining on the South Fork of Long Island. I immediately burst into tears and in between sobs, told Dennis that I would call Stephen and look after him.

Making that call was exceedingly painful, but Stephen and I did the best we could to comfort each other. I called Dennis and told him that, given the horrendous circumstances, Stephen was doing as well as could be expected.

When I spoke to Jon, he told me that Carolyn had named him as her successor, but that he had to wait to hear from Bob Bakish, the CEO of CBS, to see if they would follow her wishes. They did, and Jon accepted the job.

In the meantime, Stephen had to deal with the double whammy of losing his beloved wife of 45 years and dealing with all the grim responsibilities surrounding her death. We were on the phone back and forth about funeral arrangements and such. In a way, this kept Stephen occupied with the tiresome, mundane details of death, rather than mourning his dear departed partner.

It took me days of intermittent misery to come to grips with Carolyn's sudden demise, so it is unimaginable to think of what Stephen was going through. But Stephen is a rational person, and he was incredibly good at masterminding all the daunting details of her death.

Since then, Stephen and I have seen each other at least once a week, and we speak frequently on the phone. He has been through some very trying times, but I think he would agree that he is coming along very well.

Carolyn's death made my job as consigliere more prominent, at least initially. Jon and I got along beautifully from day one, and the tragic circumstances made us even more fully absorbed.

Jon is incredibly responsive, thoughtful, instinctive, smart, and very funny. His staff often asks me, "When does he sleep?" Beats me. But ask him a question and you will have an answer within no time. In that sense, we are very similar. Once I complained that a personnel issue was taking too long. His response was, "Not everyone moves at our speed."

I have brought them many projects, some of which are confidential, except Pope Francis's *Let Us Dream*, written with Austen Ivereigh, a cherished author of mine. I was also deeply involved in putting together the collaboration between Louise Penny and Hillary Clinton. This was pure pleasure dealing with David Gernert, Louise's agent, Robert Barnett, Hillary's representative, and Louise herself, who became a friend when I was still at Holt.

Working for Jon has been a privilege and, even at my advanced age, I have learned much from this hugely talented publishing mastermind. First, I am very impressed at how thoughtful Jon is. We both move at a quick clip, but along the way he is far more able than I am to view a situation reflectively. I thought I could handle having many balls in the air at once. Jon can handle far more. Perhaps most significantly, Jon has learned that as CEO, he has to step away from things—a great lesson for me as a supreme control freak.

19
MY CHECKERED CAREER
. . . AS AN AUTHOR

I find it strangely ironic that I, as a book publisher and former journalist, have managed to extricate myself from five potential book projects involving me as the author.

The first was in the late 1980s when I was approached by the literary agent Irene Goodman to write a biography of the great mezzo-soprano Marilyn Horne. I wrote an extensive proposal but withdrew it when Irene told me what the advance would be. Much too low for the time and work involved.

I gave my proposal to the author Jane Scovell, who wrote that book and a second one about Marilyn. They became inseparable pals, and I am delighted to report that Marilyn and I formed a relationship as well. I have always thought that of the myriad opera singers I have come to know, the only one I could imagine being close to was Marilyn, and I was right. Jane and I have always been great pals, much more so since the death of Cynthia. They were inseparable.

The other book projects had much less happy endings. I actually entered into a contractual agreement to write a history of the New York City Opera. I did reams of interviews, which I enjoyed and was good at, but my heart wasn't into doing all the historical digging necessary to get to the essence of this complicated and stormy backstory. (I published *Mad Scenes and Exit Arias* by Heidi Waleson, in 2017, which tackled the same story with much more finesse and style than I would have brought to it.)

The other books all involved superstar conductors, and I would have been a credited ghost. The first was with Erich Leinsdorf, whom I knew from my days at Boston University when he was music director of the Boston Symphony Orchestra. He was also a longtime client of Cynthia's, so we had a double connection.

Leinsdorf was smart and could be very entertaining but very nasty when crossed. We did do some preliminary work, but the arrangement fell apart because we could not agree on contractual issues. Much later, Leinsdorf wrote the book himself for Yale University Press, and Cynthia did a bang-up job publicizing it. We continued to see Leinsdorf and his second wife, Vera, until they left the States. I always referred to them as Annina and Valzacchi, the two poisonous mischief-makers in *Der Rosenkavalier*.

The next maestro was Zubin Mehta, whom I had interviewed for the *Times*. The idea was brokered by the great record and opera impresario Terry McEwen. But it wasn't to be because I found Mehta to be a jerk; he once actually insisted that I work with him while he was being massaged and, worse, that I join him for a schvitz in the steam room. Perhaps Zubin had spent too much time in Hollywood while he was the music director of the Los Angeles Philharmonic.

To guarantee this project would be stillborn, I adopted a new, obnoxious personality, which worked like a charm.

"Terry, I can't work with this guy," Zubin whined to McEwen. "We have barely started and hate each other already." Bravo, maestro.

The third doomed project never got much beyond the idea stage. My dear friend and colleague Jonathan Galassi, publisher of the literary powerhouse Farrar, Straus & Giroux, offered me a dream project: *How to Listen to Music* by James Levine and Stephen Rubin.

I knew Jim from when I interviewed him on his Met debut, and realized the brilliance of this idea because no one could speak about music more thoughtfully and astutely, to say nothing of accessibly, than James Levine. Perhaps only Leonard Bernstein could trump him.

But timing wasn't with us. Jonathan's offer occurred at the time when Jim's horrible physical ailments led to his resignation as the music director of the Boston Symphony. This was also the time when rumors started spreading about sexual harassment charges against him.

Thanks to the intervention of Jim's manager, Ronald Wilford, who was very keen on this project, Jim and I met, but there was just too much going on in the conductor's life for him to commit to such a lengthy undertaking.

Looking back on all these failed endeavors, I have to honestly admit that as a publisher, I know how much work goes into these books and do not think this is really how I want to spend my time.

I wrote *The New Met in Profile* in 1974. It was essentially a collection of my published articles, to which I added a handful of new ones and a very controversial introduction, which the *Times* reprinted. Schuyler Chapin, then general manager of the Met, never spoke to me again. My only other book involvement was with my lengthy article on Luciano Pavarotti for *The Tenors*.

20
LADIES' MAN

I often ask myself why it is that in both my personal and professional lives I am always attracted to women with gargantuan-sized personalities. I surely married one of the most outspoken, brutally honest people I have ever encountered, and I never for one second regretted it. The same is true professionally. I cannot honestly say all these relationships were as smooth-sailing as my marriage, but I would never change any of them either. Here, in brief snapshots, are my rogues' gallery of spectacular, monumental women.

Carolyn Reidy

Publishing is one of those rare industries where competitors often embrace one another. I have always considered it one of my responsibilities to check out the competition. I have had a long line of close friends who ran competing houses, starting in the 1980s with Phyllis Grann, when we spoke every morning at 8:30 a.m., and continuing throughout my career. Without a doubt, my closest pal among the many rivals was Carolyn Reidy, who was the CEO of Simon & Schuster since 2008 before dying tragically of a heart attack in 2020.

Carolyn and I were intimate friends for more than three decades. Curiously, it took my joining S&S in 2020 for me to realize what a powerful, motivational CEO Carolyn was. Sure, I should have known how tremendous she was, but it really helps to see things up close.

When I watched her first virtual town hall early in the pandemic era, the ease with which she comported herself, the way she anticipated almost all the questions her staff might ask, and the brutal candor with which she answered those questions, floored me. Carolyn was the quintessential corporate animal, yet her good nature, warmth, sense of humor, and affability, plus her no-nonsense approach and often shocking honesty, made her a captivating leader. Her staff genuinely loved her.

So did I. For three decades we confided in each other on matters both professional and personal. This was the decidedly weird aspect of our relationship; despite being fierce competitors, we never, ever betrayed each other. Nor did we ever worry we would. It was all a matter of trust. Supreme trust.

Carolyn had very little patience for what she considered stupid or time wasting. This admirable trait was tested to the extreme during the ridiculous period when the Department of Justice sued five publishers and Apple, accusing them of colluding to fix prices on e-books.

Carolyn and I had regular dinners in the Hamptons, where we both had homes, and we gossiped to a degree that might have shocked our legal counsels, to say nothing of the DOJ. We were both scrupulous about reporting our meetings, as we were required to do under the legal settlement. I remember once John Sargent, Macmillan's CEO, telling me that Carolyn had called him, and he had to cut her short in midsentence and tell her it was out of the question for them to continue talking. Carolyn was redoubtable for sure.

Despite all outward signs to the contrary, Carolyn was a private person who liked nothing more than luxuriating in her beach house or her beloved flat in Paris. These retreats were special because she could be alone with her favorite soul mate, her husband Stephen.

They had known each other since college and were together for half a century, married 45 of those years. They were an exemplary couple and were so at ease with each other, they led a somewhat insular existence. In all the years I dined with them, I can count on one hand those occasions where other people were present. This is not a complaint. I was delighted to have them all to myself, and surely elated to eat Stephen's gastronomic triumphs. I will never forget when a colleague asked Carolyn what she liked most about working remotely, and without missing a beat, she said, "having my husband fix me lunch." Carolyn knew her priorities.

On a purely selfish level, even though I have Carolyn no more as my chief confidante and dear pal, I still have Stephen as my friend. And I am blessed to have him. But there is a giant hole in my heart where Carolyn used to be.

Kitty Kelley

I first met the fearless and tenacious coquette Kitty Kelley when she delivered her magnum opus on Frank Sinatra, *His Way*, to Bantam in 1985. I will admit that I had not read her previous books on Jacqueline Onassis and Elizabeth Taylor, so I was totally unprepared for the myriad joys of mean-spirited bliss I was to experience reading the manuscript before the lawyers got their hands on it.

I have what I call the "public menace test" for books of this sort. *His Way* passed it better than anything since Albert Goldman's *Elvis*.

There was something so startling on almost every page of *His Way* that the reader became a public menace, having to share it with whomever was in earshot. I was so gobsmacked by the revelations in Kitty's book that my wife told me in no uncertain terms to either shut up or go elsewhere.

I had nothing to do with the publication of *His Way*, but I did get to see Kitty a bit and began a harmless flirtatious relationship with her that continues to this day. When I read her mind-bogglingly nasty biography of Nancy Reagan, I was in the Caribbean and sent her a genuinely extravagant mash note. Finally, in 1999 we joined forces to publish *The Family: The Real Story of the Bush Dynasty*.

To understand the indomitable Kitty Kat, as I love to call her, you have to acknowledge that she is a tireless reporter who has never been successfully sued. You also have to accept the fact that she is at her best when she has a subject she can skewer. Fair and balanced is not in her repertory.

I consider *The Family* one of Kitty's best books. She had a fine time with all the Bushes but failed to get headlines on W. Ironically, a decade later when I published *Decision Points*, I really enjoyed dealing with the former president. Kitty got a lot right about the frat boy Bush, but one of her most devastating discoveries had to go unpublished. She had heard of an incident at Yale that involved anti-semitism by the young Bush, but sadly oped not to publish it because her source was afraid not to go on the record.

When it came time to do her next book, she was determined to tackle Oprah Winfrey. I told her this was a terrible idea because Oprah's audience wasn't interested in reading negative things about their saintly hero. My staff, to a person, were dead set against it too, one or two even threatening to resign if we published it.

When I reported this to Kitty, she went nuclear. I tried to reason with her, but there was no way she would listen. She refused to speak to me for quite a while. The book was published and did modestly compared to her previous endeavors.

We finally kissed and made up, and I continued to see her socially on Long Island in the summers. There is no one who is more entertaining, and I will always adore her. We discussed many other ideas, but could never arrive on something both of us believed in. One thing is for sure: I believe in her.

Marilyn Horne

I have always thought that of the myriad opera singers I have come to know, the only one I could imagine being close to was Marilyn, and I was right.

She is most formidably a diva, but Marilyn is also forthright, funny, opinionated, and exceptionally intelligent.

She is widely engaged in the world at large as opposed to so many superstars who live exclusively in the bubble of opera. By that I mean football games, game shows, popular TV. She conquered the death sentence that is normally associated with pancreatic cancer. I watched from the sidelines and she was heroic. I have rarely seen such fierce determination. Of course her control and iron will did not really surprise me. One cannot sustain the level of excellence she has had throughout a long career without masterful discipline.

I underwrote a chair in Marilyn's name for the study of voice at Oberlin, which gave us both great pleasure. When the Kent, Connecticut, public library asked me to interview Marilyn for a very starry series they have, we jumped at the chance. She was enchanting and tremendously at ease. A year later we took the show on the road to Oberlin, where I surprised her with the question, "Is it true you cannot have sex before a performance?" Without missing a beat, she responded, "Depends on the sex." Then we did a benefit for the San Francisco Conservatory of Music at the home of Ann and Gordon Getty.

Marilyn is unquestionably one of the greatest vocalists of the twentieth century. Her mezzo-soprano has an amazing range and a formidable agility. She lives in the worlds of Rossini, Bellini, Donizetti, and other composers of florid music, but listen to her capture the emotions in a Mahler song, or the humor in songs by American composers, Broadway show tunes, and even occasionally Verdi. One night at the Met after a performance of Amneris in

Aida, she informed me in no uncertain terms that no one ever sang this part with such bel canto finesse. No argument there.

I have seen her master classes and private lessons and marveled how in one lesson she transformed good students into better ones. Marilyn is one of the great teachers because her technique is rock-solid, and she is able to verbalize the basics of good singing. I remember I once commented on how much I liked the tenor Rolando Villazon. She agreed but said his technique worried her. Years later he was having formidable vocal problems.

Marilyn has totally reveled in her fabulous career and celebrity, but she has given back to the profession more than any other contemporary singer. It is impossible not to be enchanted by the homegrown diva from Bradford, Pennsylvania.

Phyllis Grann

When I began to coauthor Writers Bloc's publishing column, I made it one of my first assignments to court the most remote source in the book business. Phyllis Grann was not only at the time the resolute, powerful CEO of Putnam, she was the mother of three children, devoted wife to a prominent oncologist, and denizen of Westport, Connecticut. She used this familial and geographic situation as an excuse to regularly avoid cocktail parties and book launches, the perfect breeding ground for hungry journalists to curry favor.

Despite these barriers, I managed to get Phyllis not only to trust me as a reporter, but to become a professional friend. It was when I was at Bantam that we began to speak every morning at 8:30. My leader at that time, Jack Romanos, warned me that this state of affairs would come to no good, that Phyllis would steal my authors, pick my brain, and generally take advantage of my inexperience. He could not have been more mistaken.

I think Phyllis needed a pal she could trust who didn't work for her, and I surely wanted to partake of the wisdom of a player I admired both for her publishing as well as corporate acumen. I do not know whether she was better as a savvy pirate, especially of established authors, or as a masterful, often ruthless CEO. It was she who masterminded Penguin's purchase of Putnam.

When Marjorie Scardino, then the CEO of Penguin's parent company, made the foolish mistake of sacking her, they lost both a fabulous editorial mind and a pugnacious CEO.

When Peter Olson pursued her to come to Random House as his second in command, Phyllis blundered uncharacteristically by accepting a job with no one reporting to her. To make matters considerably worse, Peter stopped talking to her the minute she was on board. Such was Phyllis's unhappiness and paranoia, she even accused me of betraying her. No way. She lasted six months. Phyllis is not fun under most circumstances, but she is particularly ornery when despondent.

Eventually Phyllis phoned me and said what she really wanted was to become a senior editor. I told her she was out of her mind, but she insisted. When I informed Bill Thomas and Michael Palgon of her desire, they were aghast. I made them give me a list of reasons why this was a terrible idea, took Phyllis to lunch, and laid out their objections. She parried every point and was soon on board.

Net-net it was a great association, but getting there was difficult. First, she and Bill Thomas were combative with each other, despite their respecting each other's accomplishments. I also had to have a very unpleasant conversation with Phyllis about her disruptive behavior at meetings and to remind her that she wasn't in charge, I was. She stormed out of my office in tears, and I never had another problem.

Ultimately, she brought Doubleday Tina Brown, Michael Wolff, Jeffrey Toobin, and Sally Jenkins, among many others. And it was a luxury for me to have a trusted advisor literally next door. Phyllis is a total pro and has such a wide range of experience, I could only benefit from her counsel. Most important, she played out the final act of a storied career in reasonable contentment.

Tina Brown (and Her Men)

Ed Victor, Tina Brown's longtime agent, rang me one day at Holt to offer me *Media Beast*, Tina's memoir. I immediately called Gail Rebuck to see if she would be my UK partner in publishing Tina's book, and the three of us had wonderfully intelligent conversations, particularly about the feminist aspect of her dealing with all her male bosses, especially Si Newhouse, who stopped talking to her when she decamped from the *New Yorker* to join Harvey Weinstein in creating *Talk* magazine. "What was I?" Tina asked. "His goddamned mistress?!"

Gail and I were easily convinced, and we paid $2 million for world rights to *Media Beast*. But knowing how Tina, the quintessential, brilliant magazine editor, would always find an excuse not to work on the book, Ed and I tracked her relentlessly at lunches and breakfasts. When she founded Women in the World, it literally sucked the oxygen out of the air, and her book writing suffered.

Eventually, Ed called me to say that Tina would not deliver *Media Beast* but instead would submit *The Vanity Fair Diaries*, immediately acknowledging that the new book would not be valued at what we paid for *Media Beast*, but I should read it, and then we will talk.

Luckily Tina had kept copious diaries when she was refashioning *Vanity Fair*. So there was a genuine immediacy to the pages. Then, of course, she recharged those entries and they were powerful and alluring. After fierce, unresolved negotiations, Ed and I could not reach a financial agreement, and he took the project to two other publishers on the hunt for more money. He failed and came back to say that he accepted Holt's offer. I gave them a $100,000 "welcome home" bonus and we were back in business.

The diaries were irresistible. Tina spent hours in the office working with designer Meryl Levavi from 9 to 5 daily on the photo layouts. When she finally signed off on them, I marched into Meryl's office and said, "You must be relieved."

"Working with Tina was the greatest experience of my career," she said.

That's pretty much how everybody at Holt felt. Tina could be demanding and often sent text messages completely at odds with emails and vice versa, but her cool charm, relentless devotion to the project, and considerable smarts trumped her being a garden variety pain in the ass.

I was on Tina's case about a book to follow the diaries. She was slippery as could be but finally decided she wanted to write the ultimate book about Monica Lewinsky called something like *The Little Blue Dress That Changed the World*. We all tried to dissuade her from this path, acknowledging that she would write a brilliant book but that Clinton fatigue would greatly hamper sales. We wasted months arguing back and forth.

I kept on pressuring her to return to the royals, particularly the younger ones. When Meghan Markle single-handedly rewrote the history of the Windsors, Tina became convinced as well.

Meanwhile, during all of this, Ed passed away. I spoke with Eric Simonoff, now Tina's agent, who said his new client wanted a million dollars to write a new book about the royals. I said no but suggested she write a proposal. She did, and it was captivating. So I offered her the million, but by that point Eric had sent the proposal to other publishers. Gina Centrello asked Eric what he wanted. On a lark, he said $2 million. She said okay, and adios Tina—no good-byes, nothing. Ironically, once Meghan and Harry actually left The Firm a few years later, the book was probably worth somewhere near the absurd amount Gina paid for it.

I have no ill feelings toward Tina. We had a great ride together with *The Diana Chronicles* and *The Vanity Fair Diaries*. When people ask me what she was like as a person, I always say "a cuddly barracuda."

Sadly, her husband Harry Evans died at the age of 92 in September 2020. He had been in failing health but still displayed his trademark wit and energy. He was an irresistible, galvanic force. He reminded me of a cockney street urchin. Tina was totally dependent on him for all major and minor decisions. They may have seemed like an odd couple because of their age difference (25 years), but they were genuine soul mates. At a public event once, she lovingly looked down on him from a raised platform and cooed, "my Prince Harry." That told you all you needed to know. Harry himself once memorably quipped, "My greatest strength is reckless insensitivity to the possibility of failure."

It was an equally devastating loss for Tina when Ed passed away in 2017.

I had known Ed from my days at Bantam. Since then he had set himself up in a London office in Wardour Street, a home in a spectacular maisonette in Regents Park with a Bentley in the garage, and weekends in Sissinghurst.

Once I was at Doubleday and moved to London, we became great professional as well as personal buddies. Some of our biggest projects together were the autobiography of Eric Clapton, *The Vanity Fair Diaries*, various books by the UK TV star Andrew Marr, and a memoir by Carl Bernstein.

Ed and I were both serious party boys. He gave an annual cocktail party for hundreds of publishing folk in the Hamptons, and I gave an annual sit-down dinner for sixty. We both were liberated from this lunacy when we decided to jointly halt the expensive, time-consuming, and exhausting events and began giving smallish dinners together on Long Island, and much more ritzy events together at his storied club, the soon to be 200-year-old Garrick.

My most memorable event at the Garrick was my 75th birthday in 2016. Ed very kindly sponsored me and I had eighty-four of my closest friends for a dinner in the magnificently grand dining room. They came from the United States, Italy, France, and, of course, the United Kingdom. Doing the placement was a nightmare, but I made sure Ed had the starrier guests—Arlene and Alan Alda, Sandy and Nelson DeMille—at his end of the table.

The Garrick offers its members selections from their famed wine cellar with no markup, so the celebrants were treated to unusually fine wines. I found a stentorian tenor and a fine pianist to perform some of my favorite arias. Ed was the very grand master of ceremonies and the speakers were Jane Friedman, Robert Levine, who roasted me with affectionate abandon, and my nephew, David Rotter.

Ed had been plagued for years with leukemia, and when he was in remission for long periods, he was fine, but toward the end of his life, he was in and out of hospitals. I think it was at this period that we became closest. When he was hospitalized in the States, I visited him regularly. At his side through all of this was the love of his life, the very beautiful Carol Ryan. Intelligent, funny, and totally no-nonsense, Carol was the staunch advocate for her frail husband. She never faltered and made it much easier for the many people who were calling to wish dear Ed well.

I adore Carol, stay in touch with her and occasionally see her. Being with her always reminds me of how much I miss Ed. He was a one-off, a boy from the Bronx, who established himself as a formidable international bon vivant. Beyond these fabulous trappings, he was the loyalist, dearest pal imaginable.

In the summer of 2020, Carol visited the States and I had a small dinner for her in Westhampton. Tina joined us and it was a joy for all of us to be back together again. The only person missing, of course, was Ed. For Tina, as for me, his absence is still very painful.

Jane Friedman

I met Jane Friedman more than half a century ago, when I was the roto editor at UPI and she was a pisher in the Knopf publicity department. We took to each other immediately and eventually even socialized in the evenings, me with Cynthia, Jane with Michael Friedman, her second husband and the father of her two sons, Stefan and Bradley.

From day one I found Jane both impressive and somewhat intimidating. Jane has always known how to blow smoke better than anyone, which made her a commanding PR guru and also a bit of a prima donna personally. I don't think I have ever met anyone who was seemingly so self-assured. Until I got to know her better, her confidence, whether real or counterfeit, daunted me.

As both of our careers galloped ahead, we became closer and closer. I went to the bar mitzvahs of both her sons and got to meet her fabled mother, Ruth. I was also very much around when she had an extremely unpleasant rupture from her husband. Michael was having an affair with a friend of hers, and she herself was having a hot and heavy romance with a cowboy from Idaho. It was a sordid version of *The Big Chill*.

In 1990, when I took over Doubleday, Jane's boyfriend joined Bantam Books. So we were corporate cousins. I soon began to feel a chill every time Jane and I spoke on the phone. When I called her on it, she told me that I was not being supportive enough of her boyfriend. I told her I was so overwhelmed by my new, demanding job, I barely had time for myself. Despite my trying to reason with Jane, she was having none of it, and our relationship had a very unfortunate hiatus.

But when it was announced that Jane was becoming the global CEO of HarperCollins, I picked up the phone to celebrate this extraordinary opportunity. She was delighted to hear from me, and we sort of picked up where we left off.

She did a remarkable job at HarperCollins, raising revenues from $750 million in the red to $1.5 billion in the black. She was often dubbed imperious, but who cares? She elevated HC internationally. Her staff and authors adored her. Jane is a very persuasive, inspiring, and quite irresistible leader. She radiates positive vibes, she is warm, friendly, smart, decisive, and accessible. There is a sameness to her private and personal personas. I always love to tease her that there is no better production on Broadway than "The Jane Show."

I put on quite a Jane Show myself when I cohosted with Maria Campbell a gala celebration honoring her when she became the recently deposed CEO of HC on the posh rooftop of my West Side apartment building. When Jane walked in with her mother, she saw 80 Janes. All the participants had covered their faces with Jane masks. It was pure magic, and the look on Jane's face is something I will cherish.

Her next act was the brilliant creation of Open Road Media, the first marketing platform for ebooks, which became an instant brand. Were it not for impatient venture capitalists, Jane would still be there, but the direction they wanted to take the company was anathema to her, and she resigned, turning over her board seat to her son Stefan.

Devastatingly, in 2020 Jane's celebrated mother Ruth died, months after turning 100. She was Jane's closest friend and one of the most remarkable women I have ever met. I called her the Dowager Empress, and she loved it. She was, even at 100, often the most beautiful woman in the room. I once made the disastrous mistake of suggesting she might be even more beautiful than her daughter. I thought she would never forgive me.

There is no denying that Jane got her confidence from Ruth's unerring love and support. Ruth honestly believed that Jane was the bee's knees and she was right: Jane is singular in her charisma, generosity, kindness, and love. And I am so proud to have had her as one of my most cherished, intimate friends for more than half a century.

21
THE UNLIKELY PHILANTHROPIST

When my good friend and mentor Linda Grey died in 2000, she displayed a thoughtfulness and generosity that was the basis for a transformative change in my life.

In her will she left a bequest to the Metropolitan Opera for $25,000 in my name. I had always supported what I thought were good causes, like PBS, with small donations. But this was something else altogether, and it altered my attitude toward gift-giving dramatically. The Met helped by rigorously pursuing me for money.

Before she died I mentioned to my wife that I would like to underwrite a program for the study of classical music criticism. She loved the idea, believing, as I did, that music criticism in the States was in the doldrums. The idea was amorphous to put it mildly.

When I mentioned it to a friend of mine, he said you must meet David Stull, the dean of the Conservatory at Oberlin. I will never forget when the two of them walked into my office. It was like *Men in Black*. I grabbed for my wallet.

That day, in an hour and a half, I learned firsthand about the visionary, persuasive power of David Stull. He literally took this anarchic concept and transformed it into a viable, exciting, and beneficial project.

Between us, David and I had the connections to lure the nation's most prominent music critics—Alex Ross, Anne Midgette, John Rockwell, Heidi Waleson, and Tim Page—to become the founding Writers Panel at the biennial Institute. David got the Cleveland Orchestra, the pianist Jeremy Denk, the baroque orchestra Apollo's Fire, and the International Contemporary Ensemble, whose performance included the premiere of a new work by the Pulitzer Prize–winning composer David Lang, to become our performing partners, and we were off to the races in snowy Oberlin in 2012.

It was thrilling. Each critic gave a keynote address before the four evenings when we attended a performance. The hand-selected fellows then had to write a review on deadline for the next morning, when we broke out into small workshops. The students read their reviews, which were then criticized by their fellows and the critics. We did these sessions in public as well. The Institute culminated with the awarding of a $10,000 Rubin Prize in Music Criticism to the fellow who demonstrated exceptional promise in music criticism.

What amazed me was how well it all worked. And, much to my surprise, the critics all behaved impeccably and seemed to actually like one another. Even voting on a winner was without any tension.

When David decamped to become the president of the San Francisco Conservatory, I took the Rubin Institute along with him. Oberlin tried to persuade me to stay, but I explained that David was the brains behind our success and there was no way I was proceeding without him. They were very understanding and grateful that I would continue to support the chair for Marilyn Horne.

It was in San Francisco that the Institute grew in many significant ways.

We enlarged the critics to include Joshua Kosman of the *San Francisco Chronicle*. We added jazz to our program and coaxed the great Gary Giddins to join our Writers Panel.

Perhaps most significantly, in 2016 the Institute teamed up with the Ann and Gordon Getty Foundation to provide financial support for newspapers across the nation, which were either sacking their music critics or were only using freelancers, in order to advance and maintain quality discourse on music. The program offered to pay 85 percent of the cost of staff or freelancers with the news outlets retaining complete editorial control over assignments and content. This joint financial model was responsible for about 180 articles in 2019 at such diverse newspapers as the *Boston Globe*, the *Minnesota Star Tribune*, the *Pittsburgh Post-Gazette*, the *Seattle Times*, the *Toronto Star*, the *Dallas Morning News*, and the *Chicago Tribune*, among many others.

For the 2020 Institute, which was postponed because of the pandemic, we enlarged our critics to further include our first-ever editor, Janice Page, who is in charge of culture for the *Washington Post*; Zachary Woolfe of the *New York Times*; Steve Smith, formerly of *National Sawdust*; and Natasha Gauthier of the *Ottawa Citizen*.

It was because of this extraordinary accomplishment that I began to understand the true meaning of philanthropy and became committed to exploring more avenues of public-spirited charity.

David Stull invited me to join the board of the Conservatory, which I accepted with joy, having no idea what splendid pleasures and challenges awaited me.

I had been on boards before, but nothing like this spirited, diverse, wonderfully warm and friendly group of people. At first I was cowed by their affluence and prominence, but then realized this was Silicon Valley and was to be expected. I used to joke to myself that I had to be the poorest member of the group.

But then I ceased all this silliness and made up in work what I couldn't contribute in dollars. I was asked to join the Advancement Committee and to become chair of the Communications Committee.

What a joy to be among such multifaceted people. Watching David in action is always gratifying, but he is equaled in finesse by our board chair, the sage, even-tempered Timothy Foo, a Hong Kong real estate magnate. I became friends with a select group and we see one another at wonderfully animated lunches and dinners.

When the Conservatory planned a trip to New York, I hosted a cocktail party for them in my apartment, which was covered by the *New York Times*.

I had never been much of a fan of the city of San Francisco, but visiting there four or five times a year as the only New Yorker among them, I began to warm to the place. Essentially it is a very small town and all these eminent folks knew one another, which I discovered when I was invited to different places and was shocked to discover how many people I knew. I have rarely felt more welcome. Leave it to David to intuit how congenial we would be.

Another benefit of being in San Francisco was an opportunity to reconnect with David Gockley, the outgoing general director of the San Francisco Opera. I have known David Gockley since 1972 when he was appointed general director of the Houston Grand Opera.

Cynthia was his national PR director, and he would stay with us when he came to New York and occasionally even visited us on Long Island.

Boyishly handsome and charming when he wants to be, David is enigmatic, even to those who know him well. Friends say his sometimes remote behavior masks an essential shyness.

"He does not do the normal and expected thing," conductor Patrick Summers, who has worked intimately with David since 1998, says. "He can't. It's not where he lives. Yet, at the same time, he is enormously pragmatic and practical. He exists at the extremes of the spectrum and nowhere in the middle."

His extraordinary accomplishments at the HGO and the SFO bear out this characterization. He is that rare general director who is both a businessman and an arts administrator. At both companies he was responsible for world and American premieres, young artist development programs, simulcasts, and myriad creative endeavors.

There was a rumor he was up for the big job at the Met, but it never happened. Too bad. For all his promotional and fund-raising strengths, Peter Gelb lacks David's intimate and innate knowledge of opera. Peter has come a long way since he came to the Met, but he will always be a masterful promoter rather than a producer. David is an innovator with a glorious track record to prove his daring and farsighted vision.

It will be interesting to see how the Met returns to pre-pandemic real life. They reopened in 2021 with *Fire Shut Up in My Bones*, its first opera by a black composer, which was rapturously received. The next night they did a two-hour version of *Boris Godunov*, which also got universal acclaim, and it suddenly seemed that all was okay at the world's foremost opera house. But there is still a long way to go, especially with their dwindling, elderly audience and worrisome spotty attendance.

AFTERWORD

What matters?

Having had the opportunity to review what has been an extensive career, it always baffles me how to distinguish between quality and quantity. I once did a back-of-the-envelope tally of how many books I have published at Bantam, Doubleday, and Holt. The grand total came to about 4,000 volumes. I did the same exercise from my years as a journalist, or I should say a researcher did, and I published sixty articles for the *Arts & Leisure* section of the *New York Times* and eight longer pieces for the *Times Magazine*. As a freelancer, I wrote another sixty articles, most of which were syndicated.

The numbers in both cases are impressive, but numbers themselves are meaningless. In terms of the articles, do any of them matter? Are any of them still relevant today? I have hardly reread more than a handful, but I think I can say with reasonable confidence that the two profiles I wrote on Leontyne Price give a reader a vibrant sense of one of the greatest singers of the twentieth century and the first black superstar, whose every move, she felt, was defined by race. Or as she said, "the monkey on my back."

My chapter on Luciano Pavarotti in the book *The Tenors* also, I believe, gives a dynamic portrait of a beloved artist who was the most famous classical musician since Enrico Caruso. What it lacks is a depressing chronicle of the demise of his career.

The profile I did on Joanne Greenberg in the *Psychoanalytic Review* about her writing the seminal *I Never Promised You a Rose Garden* (under the pseudonym Hannah Green) gave me an opportunity to stretch and I think I ponied up well. Much like Price and Pavarotti, Joanne is a very willing participant in the interview process. In other words, she is great copy.

She can grasp the meaning between sanity and insanity in the most compelling terms:

"Let's contemplate Tuesday," she says. "Monday comes before it; Wednesday comes after it. The miracle of Tuesday when you know reality is that you can remember from Monday and bring what you have into Tuesday, and the stuff you do on Tuesday goes into Wednesday in an ordered fashion and has a meaning also on Wednesday. Can't you just see the headline, 'Novelist Praises Tuesday.'"

Joanne has a keen sense of humor, even at her own expense. After the publication of the article, we stayed in touch and saw each other when she occasionally came from her home in Golden, Colorado, to New York.

That's it, folks. No false modesty. There are some terrific pieces but they were for the moment, which is what most journalism is about anyway. There are a couple so marginal, I have no memory of writing them, and wonder why I ever got the assignments.

Books are different. They are meant to endure, unless they are pure fluff. First, there are the longtime authorial associations. I have had some truly meaningful ones: John Grisham, Pat Conroy, Paul Auster, Hilary Mantel, Tina Brown, and Bill O'Reilly. I have published a lot of books by Ian McEwan and Margaret Atwood and had a lovely relationship with them both, but their affiliation was to Nan Talese, who published almost every word they wrote. Wherever she went, they went.

Then there are the one-offs. My most notable one was *The Da Vinci Code*. But I am equally proud of *Like Water for Chocolate*, *The Curious Incident of the Dog in the Night-Time*, *The Devil Wears Prada*, *Decision Points*, and *Me* by Elton John.

Nan and I published *A Million Little Pieces*, a book riddled with controversy. When I was shown the jacket by the art department, I remember saying, "I hate it. But go with it." All those horrid, Technicolor pills. I never much liked the book, but I felt that we supported James Frey when his editor, Sean McDonald, who had left Doubleday, was nowhere to be found. I rather liked James.

I have written at length about my relationship with John Grisham. I published twenty-three of his books and we went on a rollicking journey together. Same with Pat Conroy. We did five books together. Paul Auster and Hilary Mantel were the loveliest part of my inheritance when I joined Henry Holt. Paul was very suspicious of me at first, but with the help of a considerable amount of malt whiskey, we developed an affectionate relationship. Actually, I adore Paul. I don't think I have ever met an author who lived as much in his own bubble as Paul does (he has no email), but once you accepted his idiosyncrasies, he is irresistible. Publishing his grand opus *4 3 2 1* was a giant challenge. But the 866-page doorstop was the bestselling of all his books.

Hilary Mantel was gracious from day one. We were very aggressive about her winning the Booker award for *Wolf Hall*, and even though she was ill, she lent herself to publicity when she could. When *Bring Up the Bodies* won a second Booker, we went crazy and Hilary played along. Publishing *The Mirror and the Light* was complicated by her British publisher, Fourth Estate, but Hilary was always the sunniest, kindly, lovely person and a joy and an honor to publish.

I have said quite enough about and Bill O'Reilly and Tina Brown.

Like Water for Chocolate is a wonderfully original, magic realist novel. When we decided to go for broke with a bestseller campaign, I think a lot of our colleagues thought we were nuts. A first novel from Mexico? Yup. And we did it.

The Curious Incident of the Dog in the Night-Time is an audaciously free-spirited journey into the mind of Christopher, an autistic teenager, who is supremely literal and logical but is incapable of emotion. When Christopher is accused of murdering a neighbor's dog, his brilliant mind goes into overdrive as he decides to find the killer employing the techniques of literature's most rational sleuth, Sherlock Holmes. The result is unlike anything I have ever read: funny, heartbreaking, a mystery, and an introduction to an unforgettable character whose brilliance is blunted by his inability to fathom feelings. The book is perfect. Of how many novels can one say that?

I suppose thanks to the terrific film, *The Devil Wears Prada* has entered the zeitgeist. It is a book that is not brilliantly written but captures to perfection the madcap world of Condé Nast at the time it was still a toy box.

Its portrait of Anna Wintour from what I understand is perceptive. When I knew Anna minimally from my days at *Vanity Fair*, I found her smart and fun. She surely handled us wisely when the news was out about the book. A Condé Nast lawyer called Random House's chief legal counsel and said, "Anna wants you to know that she cares a lot about her children." Great tactical move on her part. We parted company with Lauren Weisberger when we found the proposal for her second book sorely lacking. She has been published successfully. But what fun to have her seminal work.

Acquiring George W. Bush's memoir made me public enemy no. 1 among my more liberal friends and colleagues. I couldn't care less. Bush was a joy to deal with, and when I left Random House prior to its publication, the former president wrote me a lovely, heartfelt, handwritten note. Barbara Bush, the silver fox as she was affectionately called, taught all her kids impeccable manners. I always knew the book would sell well, but if one had predicted 3 million copies, even I would have balked.

When I finished the thirty-seven-page proposal for Elton John's memoirs, I called John Sargent and told him we had to buy this book. When he read the pages, he immediately sent them to our owner, Stefan von Holtz-brinck, and he was soon on board as well. It's the best proposal of its sort I have ever read.

As is the book. Even though Elton worked with a brilliant collaborator from the *London Times*, he totally lent himself to the project, and the voice on the pages is uncannily his. It is funny, profane, brutally candid, wickedly dishy, poignant, and completely believable.

As celebrities go, Elton is okay, perhaps living in a time when he was a much bigger star than he is now, but like anyone who has seen his farewell concerts will acknowledge, he may be ravaged and overweight, but the energy level is as brawny and vigorous as ever.

I find it wonderfully fulfilling that someone like myself, who really is not much committed to pop music, has published two of the best pop music memoirs, by Eric Clapton and Elton John.

In Rodgers & Hammerstein's *South Pacific*, the character Nellie Forbush sings early on in the show that she is "A Cockeyed Optimist." My friend Phyllis Grann often referred to me affectionately as Nellie. Guilty as charged. There is no denying that I am not only sanguine, I also have a steady, good-humored disposition. None of this tranquility is ever to be confused with naiveté. I know my optimistic demeanor often annoys people, but it is who I am. I think in part it accounts for some of my success. Most of my colleagues embraced, perhaps somewhat reluctantly, my gusto.

As I look back, it amazes me how many extraordinary opportunities seem to have fallen into my lap. I know I was pushy, cheeky, even audacious at times, but there was never a master plan, a stratagem. Just optimism.